UNDERSTANDING AND PREVENTING
SUICIDE

UNDERSTANDING AND PREVENTING
SUICIDE
New Perspectives

By

DAVID LESTER, PH.D.

Professor of Psychology
Richard Stockton State College
Pomona, New Jersey

CHARLES C THOMAS • PUBLISHER
Springfield • Illinois • U.S.A.

Published and Distributed Throughout the World by

CHARLES C THOMAS • PUBLISHER
2600 South First Street
Springfield, Illinois 62794-9265

© *1990 by* CHARLES C THOMAS • PUBLISHER

ISBN 0-398-05709-5

Library of Congress Catalog Card Number: 90-11177

With THOMAS BOOKS *careful attention is given to all details of manufacturing
and design. It is the Publisher's desire to present books that are satisfactory as to their
physical qualities and artistic possibilities and appropriate for their particular use.*
THOMAS BOOKS *will be true to those laws of quality that assure a good name
and good will.*

Printed in the United States of America
SC-R-3

Library of Congress Cataloging-in-Publication Data

Lester, David. 1942–
    Understanding and preventing suicide : new perspectives / by David
Lester.
        p.   cm.
    Includes bibliographical references.
    Includes index.
    ISBN 0-398-05709-5
    1. Suicidal behavior.   2. Suicidal behavior—Social aspects.
3. Suicide—Prevention.   I. Title.
        [DNLM: 1. Suicide.   HV 6545 L6415u]
RC569.L48   1990
616.85′8445—dc20
DNLM/DLC
for Library of Congress   90-11177
                                                                            CIP

For Bijou

PREFACE

Seven perspectives are presented in this volume for understanding and preventing suicidal behavior. Although elements of some of these views have appeared in recent years, only two (individualistic positivist and social control) have any substantial parallels in standard suicide theorizing. Two of the perspectives are completely new. Virtually no consideration has been given by suicidologists to social reaction and social conflict.

We are not arguing here that these perspectives will assume great importance in the future. Rather, we are suggesting that consideration of those presented here may stimulate new research into the etiology of suicidal behavior. We have tried to illustrate the potential of these perspectives by illustrating their implications for prevention. It was readily apparent, first of all, that the perspectives do indeed suggest new strategies for preventing suicide, ranging from community action programs to setting up social networks for suicidal people.

Second, it is also apparent that they provide a rational for primary prevention, preventing the appearance of suicidal behavior in people rather than intervening once the people have become suicidal. Again, this leads to the realization that suicidologists have neglected primary prevention.

Armed with the information presented in this book, we may move far toward understanding and preventing suicide in the twenty-first century.

D.L.

CONTENTS

Contents   xi

UNDERSTANDING AND PREVENTING
SUICIDE

Chapter 1

INTRODUCTION

This book is concerned with how our understanding of suicide would be furthered if we viewed suicide *from a criminological perspective.* The words here are critical.

The thesis of this book is *not* that suicide is a crime or that it should be a crime. Far from it. However, scholars seeking to understanding criminal behavior have proposed a number of theories over the years, theories which also have implications for prevention. The aim of this book is to see whether these theories have any applicability to suicidal behavior, both in furthering our understanding of suicide and in seeking new ways to prevent suicide.

Why should this task be necessary?

The Failure of Suicide Theory

Psychology

I have recently reviewed the literature on suicide from several perspectives. From the psychological perspective, I noted (Lester, 1988a) that none of the major theorists who have contributed to the discipline ever focussed on suicide. Freud, whose work was most seminal to the discipline, did of course mention suicide, but his ideas on the topic were not collected together systematically until Litman (1967) undertook the task. After Freud, few theorists have mentioned suicide, even in passing.

Psychology in America quickly became empirical, demanding individual studies of subjects. In addition, preference was given to the study of phenomena which could be artificially simulated in the laboratory. The preferred method for psychological research is the experiment, in which the experimenter manipulates the independent variables to explore their effect on some dependent variable. As a result, the vast majority of psychological research has been conducted on the undergraduate student and the rat, both easily utilized for laboratory experimental designs (Lester, 1969).

3

Suicide is not amenable to this preferred technique of study. The suicide is dead and no longer available for study. It is hard to conceive of a laboratory analog for suicidal behavior, nor one that could be studied in animals. Furthermore, it would be considered unethical to manipulate experimental conditions so as to produce self-destructive behavior in people.

In course content, the course most clearly pertinent to suicide is Abnormal Psychology, the study of psychological disturbance. In this course, the orientation has always been tied to diagnosis, closely following decisions made by the American Psychiatric Association. Abnormal Psychology textbooks are almost always oriented around the *Diagnostic and Statistical Manual* of the American Psychiatric Association. Thus, in Abnormal Psychology textbooks, suicide is often mentioned only as an afterthought in a chapter on affective disorders, where there may be a section on suicide that might be suitable for a Sunday newspaper magazine section.

A perusal of textbooks for Theories of Personality reveals a complete absence of any references to suicide. The major journals in psychology are no better. Only occasional articles appear, and often they have methodological flaws since the editors and reviewers have so little expertise in the field of suicidology (see Lester [1988a] for several examples).

Psychiatry

Psychiatry has shown several trends in recent years which bode ill for the study of any behavior. First, the trend in the diagnostic system has away from causes and toward symptoms. The first two versions of the *Diagnostic and Statistical Manual* of the American Psychiatric Association had a strong Freudian emphasis which at least had the merit of implying causes for the behaviors. The more recent revisions have avoided any causal elements and classify the disorders only on the basis of symptoms. Thus, a paranoid schizophrenic is so labelled regardless of whether the cause might be a genetic defect in the levels of dopamine and norepinephrine in the brain (the biochemical perspective), strong repressed homosexual desires (the Freudian perspective), or inappropriate labelling by the the family members and psychiatrist (as well documented by R. D. Laing).

A second recent trend is the current emphasis on biochemical explanations of psychiatric disorder. To be sure, there are probably biochemical (and therefore genetic) inputs into the etiology of disturbed behavior (Lester, 1988b). But to expect to be able to reduce the rich diversity of human behavior (normal and abnormal) into the operation of a few neurotransmitters is as absurd a reductionism as the attempt by behaviorists to reduce the explanation of all human behavior to classical and operant conditioning.

Sociology

Sociological studies of suicide have been much more productive. One of the important theorists in early sociology, Emile Durkheim (Turner and Beeghley, 1981), devoted a book to the topic (Durkheim, 1897). This conferred a respectability on the topic, and the concepts which Durkheim proposed as underlying social causes of suicide (social integration and social regulation) have become core concepts for future students of suicide.

Deviant behavior is a standard course in sociology departments, and suicide is properly included in the range of the course. The leading sociology journals publish articles on suicide that are methodologically sound, important for a theoretical understanding of suicide, and important empirical contributions.

However, Durkheim has become far too important in the field. Almost every article bases its theoretical or empirical contribution on Durkheim's ideas. New theories proposed since Durkheim can be seen as simple extensions of Durkheim's ideas, but I have had the experience of articles which cite these later theories being accepted only on condition I cite Durkheim instead. It has proven extremely difficult for sociologists to break away from the confines of his influence even though other theoretical possibilities abound as I have shown (Lester, 1989a).

Preventing Suicide

Efforts at preventing suicide appear to have failed. Despite all of the efforts over the last thirty years, the overall American suicide rate continues to remain stable at about 12 suicides per 100,000 people per year. Occasionally, alarming increases are noted: American Indians in the 1970s, adolescents in the 1980s, and now the elderly perhaps in the 1990s.

Prevention techniques remain unchanged. The rapid growth of suicide prevention and crisis intervention centers in the the 1960s and 1970s has not been shown to have had any beneficial impact (Lester, 1989b).

The effectiveness of individual psychiatric and psychotherapeutic treatment also remains unproven for suicide prevention.

The profession remains resistant, however, to considering other techniques for prevention. Clarke and Lester (1989) have advocated techniques from the field of public health, arguing that restricting access to lethal methods for suicide might well reduce the suicide rate (yet there is no sign that the Golden Gate Bridge would ever be fenced in to prevent people jumping from it, for example) or that public education *against* suicide might be more effective than current suicide awareness programs (Lester, 1989c).

Thus, the field of suicide prevention appears to be stuck in the ruts in which it has been running for twenty years. Indeed, examination of the Proceedings of the Annual Meeting of the American Association of Suicidology shows that many of the articles are similar to those presented twenty years ago.

A Source of New Perspectives

Where might the field of suicide draw new perspectives? As mentioned above (and as indicated by the focus of this volume, of course), the aim of the present book is to suggest that theories of crime and delinquency might provide a set of new perspectives for understanding and preventing suicide.

Crime and delinquency has attracted a great deal of attention from sociologists so that it has become a major field with its own professional associations and journals. Furthermore, it has been truly an interdisciplinary field, attracting scholars from many disciplines. And finally, the severity of the problem of crime in modern society has led to a great deal of thought and expenditure on efforts to prevent crime.

As we shall see in this volume, it is easy to identify at least seven major theories of crime and delinquency. Some of these have parallels in the study of suicide, but others do not. These latter theories, therefore, suggest areas of theorizing that suicidologists might profitably consider.

In addition, the field of criminology has devoted a great deal of thought to juvenile crime, so that courses and textbooks are devoted specifically to juvenile delinquency. This heavy emphasis on criminal behavior in the young has also led criminologists to focus a great deal on *early* identification of and intervention in criminal behavior, an orientation that should prove to be useful for suicidologists.

Thus, it is with a great deal of enthusiasm that I present this work. My hope is that it will draw students of suicide out of their narrow disciplinary boundaries and stimulate creative theorizing and prevention efforts in the future.

Completed Suicide and Attempted Suicide

Since in this volume we will consider both suicidal acts in which the person dies (completed suicide) and where the person survives (attempted suicide), it is necessary in this introductory chapter to consider the relation between these two behaviors.

Attempted suicide has an ambiguous position as a topic for study. Although attempts at suicide are at least eight times more common than deaths from suicide, completed suicide remains the major focus of interest for suicidologists.

Since the subjects for researchers interested in completed suicide are deceased, and so unavailable for psychological testing and psychiatric study, suicidologists have turned to the study of attempted suicides as substitute subjects (Neuringer, 1962).

Thus, the relationship between the behaviors of completed suicide and attempted suicide has been a concern for many years to suicidologists. The prevailing view today is that attempted suicides and completed suicides are two very different but overlapping populations. According to this view, one can learn very little about completed suicide from a study of attempted suicide, and vice versa. Lester (1970) discussed the evidence that had been presented relevant to this issue and pointed out that the prevailing view may be incorrect.

(1) FOLLOW-UP OF ATTEMPTED SUICIDE. Dorpat and Ripley (1967) reviewed studies that had followed-up groups of attempted suicides, and they estimated that the percentage of attempted suicides who killed themselves is between 10 and 20 percent.

(2) RETROSPECTIVE STUDIES OF COMPLETED SUICIDE. Wilkins (1967) and Dorpat and Ripley (1967) reviewed studies estimating the proportion of completed suicides who had formerly attempted suicide, and these estimates ranged from 9 to 62 percent. Lester felt that these kinds of data were not really relevant to the relationship between attempted and completed suicide. The association could be complete, and yet the two behaviors could be differently determined *or* the association could be minimal, and yet the two behaviors could have similar determinants.

(3) Differences Between Attempted And Completed Suicides. Davis (1967) reviewed studies comparing attempted suicides and completed suicides and reported that the two groups were similar on only five of the seventeen variables that he investigated. He took this to mean that the behaviors were very different. However, consider the variable of sex. Dorpat and Boswell (1963) found that the sex ratio in a sample of attempted suicides increased monotonically as the seriousness of the attempts increased. Thus, there appeared to be a continuum with respect to this variable. However, the extreme groups differed in their sex ratio from the other groups. Thus, the existence of differences between two groups does not argue against the existence of a continuum of behaviors.

(4) The Lethality Of Successive Attempts. Eisenthal et al. (1966) found no significant relationship between the lethality of early and subsequent attempts at suicide. Cutter et al. (1969), on the other hand, found that the previous attempts of male completed suicides were less lethal than their final successful attempts, but they did not report on the lethality of intermediate attempts other than the first and last attempts. Lester et al. (1978) also found that attempted suicides who later completed suicide obtained higher scores on an objective scale of suicidal intent based on the circumstances of the suicidal act for their completed suicide than for their earlier attempted suicide.

Lester (1970) noted that it would be of interest to examine the lethality and intent of each suicidal act in individuals who have made several attempts. If the lethality and intent increased monotonically with successive acts, this would support the existence of a continuum in the behaviors.

(5) The Accompaniments Of Suicidal Behavior. Callender (1968) asked students to check the instances and degrees of suicidal preoccupation that they had experienced. On the whole, people underwent the experiences of less preoccupation preceding their most serious preoccupation with suicide, and they did so in the order of seriousness. Callender felt that these lesser preoccupations constituted a necessary and integral history leading to progressively more serious preoccupations. Callender noted that the students who had attempted suicide, for example, had responded and felt when they were considering suicide intellectually just as those who have never considered suicide in any way other than intellectually. Callender concluded that suicidal experiences of all types have some common etiological sources and that minimal suicidal experiences are continuous with serious suicidal experiences in the elaboration of these sources.

Extrapolation from Attempted to Completed Suicide

Lester concluded that the prevailing view that completed and attempted suicides constitute two different but overlapping populations was not correct. It was not supported by the evidence, and it had impeded research because it implied that one cannot learn about completed suicides by studying attempted suicides and vice versa. The most tenable assumption was that suicidal behaviors fall on a continuum and that it is possible to order the different forms of suicidal behavior in terms of a dimension of lethality or seriousness. It seems likely that one can extrapolate from investigations of groups falling at some points on the continuum to groups falling elsewhere on the continuum.

Lester argued therefore that if samples of attempted suicides were to be classified by suicidal intent or the medical lethality of their suicidal action and if monotonic trends were identified from low to high intent for some target variable, then extrapolation could be utilized to describe the most seriously suicidal people of all, the completed suicides.

To illustrate this technique of extrapolation, Lester et al. (1975) classified a sample of attempted suicides by their intent to die. They found that depression scores, hopelessness scores, and variables such as the proportion leaving suicide notes increased with increasing suicidal intent. They argued that these monotonic trends could be extended to make predictions about the group with the highest suicidal intent—completed suicides.

Lester et al. (1979) followed up their sample of attempted suicides until a number of them had completed suicide. These completed suicides were found to have had high depression and hopelessness scores at the initial testing (shortly after their previous suicide attempt), as high in fact as those with the most serious intent at that time. They felt that this result gave support to the strategy of extrapolation.

In the light of the evidence reviewed above, it seems appropriate, therefore, in this volume to focus on both attempted suicide and completed suicide.

Conclusions

In this introductory chapter we have presented the rationale for considering suicide in the light of criminological theory. We hope that it will provide a source of new theoretical insights and provide new ideas for future suicide prevention efforts. We have also considered the spectrum of suicidal behaviors and argued that it makes sense, at least in this preliminary phase of investigation, to include both attempted suicide and completed suicide in our focus.

REFERENCES

Callender, W. D. A socio-psychological study of suicide-related behavior in a student population. *Dissertation Abstracts*, 1968, 28A, 3765.

Clarke, R. V., & Lester, D. *Suicide: closing the exits.* New York: Springer-Verlag, 1989.

Cutter, F., Jorgensen, M., Farberow, N. L., & Ganzler, S. Ratings of intention in suicidal behavior. Los Angeles: Los Angeles Suicide Prevention Center, 1969.

Davis, F. B. The relationship between suicide and attempted suicide. *Psychiatric Quarterly*, 1967, 41, 752–765.

Dorpat, T. L., & Boswell, J. W. An evaluation of suicidal intent in suicide attempts. *Comprehensive Psychiatry*, 1973, 4, 117–125.

Dorpat, T. L., & Ripley, H. S. The relationship between attempted suicide and completed suicide. *Comprehensive Psychiatry*, 1967, 8, 74–89.

Durkheim, E. *Le suicide.* Paris: Felix Alcan, 1897.

Eisenthal, S., Farberow, N. L., & Shneidman, E. S. Follow-up of neuropsychiatric patients in suicide observation status. *Public Health Reports*, 1966, 81, 977–990.

Lester, D. The subject as a source of bias in psychological research. *Journal of General Psychology*, 1969, 81, 237–248.

Lester, D. Relation between attempted suicide and completed suicide. *Psychological Reports*, 1970, 27, 719–722.

Lester, D. *Suicide from a psychological perspective.* Springfield, IL: Charles C Thomas, 1988a.

Lester, D. *The biochemical basis of suicide.* Springfield, IL: Charles C Thomas, 1988b.

Lester, D. *Suicide from a sociological perspective.* Springfield, IL: Charles C Thomas, 1989a.

Lester, D. *Can we prevent suicide?* New York: AMS, 1989b.

Lester, D. Public health education against suicide. *Crisis*, 1989c, 10, 181–183.

Lester, D., Beck, A. T., & Trexler, L. Extrapolation from attempted suicide to completed suicide. *Journal of Abnormal Psychology*, 1975, 84, 563–566.

Lester, D., Beck, A. T., & Narrett, S. Suicidal intent in successive suicidal actions. *Psychological Reports*, 1978, 43, 110.

Lester, D., Beck, A. T., & Mitchell, B. Extrapolation from attempted suicide to completed suicide. *Journal of Abnormal Psychology*, 1979, 88, 78–80.

Litman, R. E. Sigmund Freud on suicide. In E. S. Shneidman (Ed.), *Essays in self-destruction.* New York: Science House, 1967, 324–344.

Neuringer. C. Methodological problems in suicide research. *Journal of Consulting Psychology*, 1962, 26, 273–278.

Turner, J. H.. & Beeghley, L. *The emergence of sociological theory.* Homewood, IL: Dorsey, 1981.

Wilkins, J. Suicidal behavior. *American Sociological Review*, 1967, 32, 286–298.

Chapter 2

A CLASSICAL THEORY OF SUICIDE

The principles of the Classical School of criminology were stated most clearly by Cesare Beccaria (1738–1794) in Italy and Jeremy Bentham (1758–1832) in England.

Beccaria, a mathematician and economist, was concerned about the inconsistencies in the ways governments managed various affairs. In criminal justice, it seemed to him, judges were capricious and swayed by personal considerations. Judges had considerable power in determining sentences and often added to the punishments prescribed by law.

In his book published in Italy in 1764, Beccaria (1963) argued that a system of laws and contracts is necessary for society, but made by the legislature rather than the judges. The function of the judge should be simply to determine guilt, while the penalties should be a matter of law. He urged the establishment of a scale of crimes and punishments which takes into account only the criminal act itself and not the intent of the offender.

Beccaria saw punishment as useful, for it prevents crime. Thus, laws should be published and well learned by the people, trials should be public and speedy, and punishment should be certain and immediate. In addition, he urged the end of torture, the use of imprisonment rather than capital punishment, and better conditions for prisons. Vold (1979) classifies Beccaria's position as legal and administrative criminology.

The ideas of Beccaria were based on several ideas current in social philosophy at the time. The idea of the *social contract* held that an individual was bound to society only by his consent and, therefore, society was responsible to the citizen as well as the reverse. Individuals had rights and should lose only enough liberty as to make society viable.

Behavior was also seen as the product of free will. It was purposive and determined by hedonism. People acted so as to maximize pleasure and minimize pain. Punishment was, therefore, intended to increase the pain resulting from criminal acts. This philosophy also did not admit of extenuating personal or social consequences to excuse the offender from punishment. The punishment should fit the crime.

Beccaria was not in favor of severe punishment. Punishment, if swift and certain, need be only as severe as necessary to deter people from criminal acts.

Meanwhile in England, Jeremy Bentham, a philosopher who also studied law, was also reflecting on crime and punishment (Bentham, 1967). Classified today as a *utilitarian hedonist,* Bentham wanted to maximize the good in the society—the greatest good for the greatest number of people. Like others in the eighteenth century, Bentham believed that people were rational and would choose to maximize pleasure and minimize pain.

Bentham, like Beccaria, proposed that specific punishments assigned to each crime would increase the pain and thereby decrease the incidence of crime. The potential pain of the criminal act when the offender is caught must outweigh the potential pleasure obtained. If this is so, then the rational person will refrain from committing the criminal act.

Like Beccaria, he also eschewed severe punishment and urged that only crimes which damage society should be punished. Acts which are an offense only to morals and which do not interfere with the rights of others should not be considered criminal. Bentham also wrote on the design and management of prisons and served as an inspiration for a new type of prison administrator.

The classical position had a major impact on the criminal justice system for over a hundred years, but eventually it was replaced in the twentieth century by the view that criminals should be *treated* rather than *punished.* However, in recent years, the classical position has grown in strength again as efforts at rehabilitating criminals appear to have had little success (von Hirsch, 1976; Newman, 1983).

Modern classical theorists argue also for swift and certain punishments which do not necessarily have to be severe, punishments which are uniform and which fit the crime, and incapacitation of known chronic offenders so that they cannot commit additional crimes. Today, we see many jurisdictions imposing fixed minimum terms for certain crimes (such as dealing drugs or crimes committed with a gun) and increasing incarceration rates (which is leading at the present time to overcrowded prisons).

The Law and Suicide

Suicide has been declared criminal in the past by three great legal traditions: Roman Law, Church Law and English Law.

In England in 1809, Blackstone in his *Commentaries* argued that suicide should be punished because it is against God and King. He suggested mangling the body of the suicide and exposing it to public view as a way of preventing suicide. John Wesley, the methodist reformer, suggested in 1790 dragging the naked bodies of female suicides through the street. Desecration of the body of the suicide was meant to show how heinous the crime was (Hillman, 1964).

However, the deterrent against suicide was usually confiscation of the property of the suicide, which was forfeited to the crown. Penalties against the estate of the suicide could still be levied up until 1961 in England, and life insurance was often denied to the survivors of a suicide.

Suicide and Life Insurance

Barraclough and Shepherd (1977) noted in England that the policies of insurance companies were still inconsistent and that often the survivors received little or no compensation. In America today, the standard suicide clause is "Death from suicide within two years from the date of issue, whether the insured is sane or insane, shall limit the liability of the company to the return of the amount of premiums paid." Colorado and North Dakota set the time period as one year, New York requires that the phrase "whether the insured is sane or insane" be removed, and Missouri requires proof of intent to commit suicide at the time of insuring.

Lester (1988a) surveyed twenty American insurance companies (both large and small in size) and found that they all used the two-year time period, except for one large company which imposed only a one-year time period. One large company informed Lester that case law presumes against suicide, which makes it necessary for the insurance company to have irrefutable evidence for suicide, such as a suicide note. Since suicide notes are left by only about 40 percent of all suicides, insurance companies often pay cases which are suicide but which they cannot contest. This company also noted that many suicides are disguised, such as car crashes, and so cannot be contested. All of the companies returned the premiums for suicides within the two-year period, some with interest.

Suicide and the Law

Victoroff (1983) has reviewed the (then) current laws on suicide in the states of America. His codings are shown in Table 2.1. No state assigned criminal penalties for completed suicide, but Oklahoma and Texas assigned criminal penalties for attempted suicide.

Lester (1988b) suggested that state laws on suicide might reflect the attitudes of the people in each state on suicide. States with more punitive laws might have residents more opposed to suicide. He correlated the presence or absence of these provisions with the state suicide rates in 1980 and found no associations. Thus, state laws on suicide were not related to state suicide rates. A multiple regression analysis of the eight state law provisions accounted for only 19 percent of the variance in the suicide rates.

However, in the modern context, it is clear that suicide is not illegal or, alternatively, the penalties are rarely enforced.

Is Suicide a Rational Choice?

An Economic Approach[1]

The similarity between the analysis of some issues in economics and related issues in psychology has often been noted. For example, Lea (1978) has noted that both economics and psychology are concerned with choices, and some of the basic assumptions of theories of choice are common to both disciplines.

In particular, Lea noted that analogies exist between the paradigm of operant conditioning in psychology and demand analysis in economics. Economists call the function which relates the quantity of a commodity that is bought by a consumer to the price of the commodity the *demand curve.* Lea argued that the number of reinforcements obtained in operant conditioning is equivalent to the "quantity bought" by a subject. The schedule of reinforcement is equivalent to the "price." The schedule of reinforcement may be fixed-interval or fixed-ratio, and the variation in the size of the schedule (which interval or which ratio) parallels the price.

Lester (1988c) has proposed a learning theory for suicide. He argued that suicide is, at least in part, a learned behavior and he documented how this might be so. He examined the role that cultural norms, child-

---

1. This section was written by Bijou Yang.

Table 2.1

	A	B	C	D	E	F	G	H
State Laws on Suicide (from Victoroff, 1983)								
Alabama		x	x					
Alaska		x	x				x	
Arizona		x	x			x		
Arkansas			x					
California		x		x	x			
Colorado						x		x
Connecticut		x	x					
Delaware		x						
Florida		x					x	
Georgia				x				
Hawaii		x	x	x				
Idaho								
Illinois								
Indiana		x						
Iowa							x	
Kansas		x		x	x			
Kentucky								
Louisiana								
Maine		x						
Maryland			x					x
Massachusetts						x	x	
Michigan								
Minnesota		x					x	x
Mississippi		x				x	x	
Missouri			x			x		x
Montana		x						
Nebraska								
Nevada		x						
New Hampshire		x	x					
New Jersey				x				
New Mexico		x			x	x		
New York		x	x			x		x
North Carolina					x			
North Dakota						x		
Ohio				x				
Oklahoma	x	x		x		x		
Oregon								
Pennsylvania								
Rhode Island				x				
South Carolina								
South Dakota		x				x		
Tennessee								
Texas	x			x		x		
Utah						x		

Table 2.1 (continued)

	A	B	C	D	E	F	G	H
Vermont								
Virginia						x		x
Washington	x					x		
West Virginia						x	x	x
Wisconsin	x	x	x					
Wyoming								
Puerto Rico	x							
Virgin Islands	x							

Criminal Statutes

A   Criminal penalties for attempted suicide.
B   Criminal penalties for aiding another in committing suicide or for forming suicide pacts.
C   Statutes expressly permitting the use of reasonable force to prevent another from taking his/her own life.
D   Statutes providing criminal penalties for anyone with knowledge of a suicide who fails to immediately notify the coroner or medical examiner.

Civil Statutes

E   Statutes allowing individuals to refuse extraordinary life-support measures in certain cases. "Not a suicide" by legislative fiat.
F   Statutes that limit an insurance company's denial of payment on life-insurance or double-indemnity policy claims in cases of suicide.
G   Statutes affecting recovery of Worker's Compensation payments in cases of suicide.
H   Statutes expressly abolishing common laws of escheat or forfeiture of the land and property of suicide victims to the state.

In addition, in Texas it is a misdeamenor to threaten to commit suicide within earshot of a law-enforcement official. Alabama, California and Minnesota have criminal penalties for the accidental death of another in connection with a suicide attempt.

hood experiences of punishment, and rewards contingent upon self-harming behavior play in determining the occurrence of suicidal behavior. His analysis suggested that an economic model of suicide might be possible, since learning theory and demand analysis in economics share similarities as Lea pointed out.

In a cost-benefit analysis of suicide, committing suicide is considered to be a rational act. An individual is acting "rationally" if, given a choice between various alternatives, he selects what seems to be the most desirable or the least undesirable alternative. Economists would not judge whether suicide is a wrong, immoral or deviant act.

The decision to commit suicide depends upon the benefits and costs associated with suicide and with alternative actions. An individual will be less likely to commit suicide if the benefits from suicide decrease, the costs of suicide increase, the costs of alternative actions decrease or the benefits from alternative activities increase.

The benefits from suicide include escape from physical or psychologi-cal pain (as in the suicide of someone dying from terminal cancer), the anticipation of the impact of the suicide's death on other people (as in someone who hopes to make the survivors feel guilty), or restoring one's public image (as in the suicide of Antigone in Sophocles's play of the same name). In addition, the act itself may be enjoyable. Those who self-injure themselves by cutting their wrists sometimes report that the act of cutting relieves built-up tension and that they feel no pain.

There are several costs in committing suicide. These include the money and effort spent in obtaining the information and equipment needed for the act of suicide, the pain involved in preparing to kill oneself and in the process of committing suicide, the expected loss as a result of committing suicide such as the expected punishment predicted by most of the major religions of the world, and the opportunity costs (that is, the net gain to be expected if other alternative activities were chosen and life continued).

An individual will engage in suicide only if its benefits are greater than all of the costs mentioned above. Therefore, an economic model would suggest preventing suicide by increasing its costs or by decreasing its benefits.

Suicide can also be analyzed as if it were a commodity or a service that we purchase. However, it is immediately obvious that suicide is very different from the typical objects that we purchase. For example, when we buy an object, we pay a specific price to obtain it and then we enjoy it. Suicide results in death, and as a result we have to conceptualize our enjoyment of it quite differently.

Suicide is somewhat similar to the purchasing of health care services. In both, we pay a price to get rid of something: life in the case of suicide and sickness in the case of health care. Yet, there is a basic difference between suicide and health care, in that suicide leads to death while health care (hopefully) leads to further life. Of course, for those who believe that there will be a "life after death," suicide also leads to further life but of a different kind.

Looking at matters from a demand-side perspective, when we pur-chase a commodity (or a service), the price we pay for the commodity (or service) reflects the benefits we expect to receive from consuming that commodity. From a demand-side perspective, beef costs more than chicken because the public desires beef more, and their stronger desire for beef reflects their expectation of greater satisfaction from eating beef than from eating chicken.

In a demand-side analysis of suicide, the notion of its "price" is different from the ordinary price of a commodity. The benefit expected by a suicide is the relief of tremendous distress. Accordingly, we must use a scale of distress to measure the benefit expected by the suicidal individual. This benefit expected by the suicidal individual is reflected in the price he must pay for his suicide.

Accordingly, the demand curve is a relationship indicating the probability of committing suicide as a function of the amount of distress felt by the individual. As the amount of distress increases, the probability of committing suicide increases. The demand for suicide is, therefore, an upward-sloping curve, which is quite different from the typical downward-sloping demand curve found in most economic analyses.

On the supply side, the probability of committing suicide is related to the cost of committing suicide. The cost of committing suicide includes the cost from losing your life, collecting information about how to commit the act, purchasing the means for suicide, etc. While the latter two items have a clear-cut scale of measurement, the cost of losing life is much harder to measure. It includes at least three components, namely, the psychological fear of death, the loss of income in the future which otherwise would have been earned by the suicide, and the loss of any enjoyment that would be experienced during the rest of your "natural" life.

The higher the cost of committing suicide, the lower the probability that an individual will actually kill himself. Therefore, the supply curve should be a downward-sloping curve.

Both the demand for suicide and supply for suicide are shown in Figure 2.1. The vertical axis indicates the price (or the cost) of committing suicide, while the horizontal axis represents the probability of committing suicide. Since the probability of committing suicide is used to indicate the quantity demanded or supplied, the upper limit for this variable is one. The demand curve is an upward-sloping curve and becomes vertical when the probability of committing suicide is equal to one. The price level for committing suicide which corresponds to the point where the probability is equal to one refers to the threshold level of distress that an individual can no longer tolerate. In this situation, committing suicide becomes inevitable.

The intersection of the demand and supply curves represents an

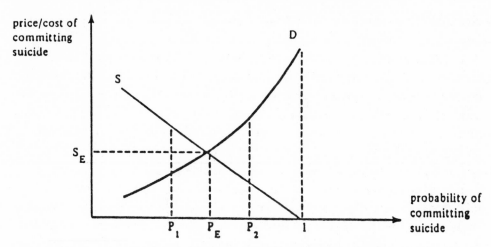

Figure 2.1. The demand and supply of suicide.

equilibrium for an individual. For that equilibrium level of distress and the corresponding costs of committing suicide there is an equilibrium probability of committing suicide. As the supply curve might intersect any section of the demand curve, the equilibrium probability of committing suicide can range anywhere from zero to one.

What needs to be determined in this demand-supply analysis of suicide is how to convert the psychological variables (level of distress and future pleasure) into measures comparable to monetary units so that an equilibrium can be obtained through equating the demand and supply for suicide.

One way to measure the level of distress is to operationalize it as to the cost of the psychological services required to eliminate the distress that the suicidal person is experiencing. Since there is a typical price for psychological services, each level of distress could be converted into a monetary measure representing the cost of psychological services needed to eliminate the distress.

This is complicated by the fact that psychological services are not always effective. Some people do not benefit from treatment. This could be taken into account by incorporating the probability of success of the treatment into the calculations, as a multiplier of the cost of treatment.

Converting future pleasure from life into monetary units is more difficult. One alternative could be to convert all of the components of the cost into subjective units, based on the ratings given by representative members of the society.

Rational-Choice Theory

Lester (1988d) cast suicide as a rational choice by examining how suicide met the conditions for Cornish and Clarke's (1986) rational-choice theory of criminal behavior. Their theory minimized the importance of internal forces in the criminal that cause him to commit crimes and over which he has little control in favor of viewing the criminal as someone who chooses to commit crimes in order to meet commonplace needs for such things as money, sex, and excitement.

Rational-choice theory assumes that criminals respond selectively to characteristics of particular offenses and to their opportunities, costs and benefits in deciding whether or not to choose an alternative crime if one becomes more difficult to commit. If one crime is no longer possible, the criminal may seek non-criminal activities and desist from further crimes of any kind, rather than displacing to some other crime.

Clarke and Lester (1989) applied this idea to the choice of method for suicide. Their research on the use of firearms, domestic gas, and car exhaust for suicide in the United Kingdom, the Netherlands, the USA and Australia persuaded them that people respond to the availability of methods for suicide in their choice of how to kill themselves and do not always switch to alternative methods for suicide when one method becomes less available. For example, as domestic gas was detoxified in England and Wales, the use of domestic gas for suicide dropped dramatically, while the use of other methods did not rise at a corresponding rate.

Lester (1988e) has shown that people view different methods of suicide quite differently. He found that the use of guns for suicide as opposed to medication was perceived as quick, painful, difficult, irreversible, dramatic, masculine and messy. Thus, if a particular characteristic of one method for suicide is critical in your choice of it as a method for killing yourself, you will not switch to an alternative method if your preferred method becomes unavailable.

In discussing opportunities for methods for suicide, Clarke and Lester listed the following as important: (1) The availability of a particular method to the individual. Does he own a car or a gun? Are high buildings easily accessible? (2) How aware is the person of particular methods for suicide and how they must be used? People may not have realized that particular pesticides can be used for suicide. Or they may not have realized how difficult it is to use the exhaust of cars equipped with emission controls. (3) What technical skills are necessary for using a particular method for suicide? For example, will the person have the necessary technical skills for disconnecting the emission control system of the car and attaching a hose to the exhaust?

Lester also considered the costs of using a particular method for suicide. He mentioned such factors as the degree of planning involved, the pain involved and the courage needed, the consequences of failure (such as disabilities and shame), and the effects after death of using a particular method (such as disfigurement).

What are the benefits of using a particular method for suicide? Some methods may be more likely to kill you (guns are more lethal than medications), spare you a prolonged period of semi-consciousness, give you scope for second thoughts, increase or decrease the chances of discovery, and create a particular image after death.

Lester went further and noted that if we make suicide more difficult, perhaps people will switch to other symptoms of psychological distress?

For example, even in suicidal behavior, people can choose between completed and attempted suicide. Broadening our concept of suicide leads us to consider behaviors such as alcohol abuse or drug abuse or even heavy smoking) which Menninger (1938) called *chronic suicide*) or self-mutilation (which Menninger called *focal suicide*). Looking further afield, potentially disturbed people may choose severe depressions, anxiety attacks both unfocussed and focussed (phobias), obsessions and compulsions, psychotic symptoms such as delusions and hallucinations, and so on. It has often been said that some people kill themselves rather than go crazy, while others go crazy rather than kill themselves.

If it be objected that psychiatric symptoms are not under our control, it should be noted that several authorities have suggested that choice of symptom may in fact occur. Scheff's (1966) labeling theory and social learning theory (Bandura, 1977) have both argued that the symptoms of psychiatric disturbance are indeed learned and that so-called psychiatric patients choose what style to adopt in their role as psychiatric patients (Braginsky et al., 1969).

In this case, we have to examine the opportunities, costs and benefits of different symptoms or behaviors. For example, for some cultures and for some people in particular cultures, suicide may be viewed as morally wrong. Thus, people who hold that suicide is morally wrong may be forced to adopt other symptoms at times of psychological distress.

In summary, Clarke and Lester have argued that suicide may be the result of a rational choice by distressed individuals and, as such, affected by consideration of the costs and benefits of the choice.

The Morality of Suicide

Sociologists have long debated whether Roman Catholicism or Protestantism is more rejecting of suicide. Recently, Simpson and Conklin (1989) have looked at correlates of national suicides and concluded that once other socioeconomic differences are taken into account, Catholic and Protestant nations have similar suicide rates. However, they showed that Islamic nations had very low suicide rates despite other socioeconomic differences.

The Koran explicitly proscribes suicide though, if the suicide is psychiatrically disturbed, modern Islamic cultures may forgive the action (Ezzat, 1983). Thus, it appears that a moral prohibition against suicide may deter people from committing suicide.

Implications for Prevention

It is not feasible to introduce punishment for suicide in the modern age. However, since there are various moral philosophies which are opposed to suicide, it would perhaps not be unreasonable to emphasize the position taken by these philosophies. The Roman Catholic Church, for example, has taken a very strong moral stand on abortion in the 1980s. A similar stand could be taken against suicide.

Lester (1989) has argued that public education about suicide differs, for example, from public education about medical diseases. In educating the public about smoking, for example, public health information has focussed on the dangers of smoking. The fact that smoking causes lung cancer and may damage the embryos of pregnant women is stressed. A recent television advertisement featured Yul Bryner, who had died from lung cancer, in a videotape made before he died in which he urged people, "Don't smoke!" Those who are vehemently opposed to smoking have in the past published shocking photographs of diseased lung tissue and heart-rending stories about persons who have suffered from lung cancer. Public education about AIDS and drug abuse are similarly strong and blunt.

In contrast, public education programs about suicide have had a very different focus. Entertaining dramas involving suicidal teenagers have appeared on television. The public has been informed on the warning clues to suicide in others. Local suicide prevention services are also advertised. This type of information is very different from that on smoking or AIDS. How might suicide education increase the apparent costs of suicide?

(1) Many people survive suicide attempts with terrible and permanent disabilities, a fact not generally known. For example, the effects of carbon monoxide poisoning include apathy, confusion and memory defects, which can be permanent. Similarly, many people survive jumping in front of a train or gunshot wounds. As one who reads the medical literature on suicide, I have frequently read about the difficulties of reconstructing the face of a suicide who survived a bullet in the head. Even the ingestion of medications, such as paracetamol which is popular in England, can lead to permanent damage to kidneys and other organs.

How might it be if someone with a grossly deformed face from a suicide attempt by gunshot or on a dialysis machine faced a camera and said "Don't do it!" as Yul Bryner did for the anti-smoking campaign?

(2) A growing body of literature has appeared on the difficulties faced by the families of suicides. Their feelings, especially of anger and guilt, are much more difficult to cope with than those felt after a natural death, and family members often face hostile neighbors and friends. Public education programs could focus on the grief and suffering caused to relatives and friends who survive those who kill themselves.

(3) Thirdly, as noted above, many religions frown upon suicide, some more strongly than others. One way to increase the costs of suicide may be to draw attention to the religious prohibition against suicide and the consequences that the would-be suicide may face in the afterlife.

Conclusions

A classical theory of suicide would stress the rationality of the act, hypothesizing that it is often based upon an accurate evaluation of the costs and benefits of suicide versus other alternatives. Suicides may be seeking to maximize pleasure or minimize pain.

Punishment for suicide may not be a feasible alternative, and there is no evidence that punishment had or did not have an effect on suicide rates. However, public education programs could easily emphasize the costs of suicide in terms of possible disfigurement, the pain caused to loved ones, and the possible consequences after death. Such information might increase the apparent costs of suicide to people, thereby making suicide a less reasonable choice for them.

REFERENCES

Bandura, A. *Social learning theory.* Englewood Cliffs, NJ: Prentice-Hall, 1977.

Barraclough, B. M., & Shepherd, D. Suicide and life insurance. *British Medical Journal,* 1977, 2, 46.

Beccaria, C. *On crimes and punishments.* Translated by H. Paolucci. Indianapolis: Bobbs-Merrill, 1963.

Bentham, J. *A fragment on government and an introduction to the principles of morals and legislation.* Edited by W. Harrison. Oxford: Basil Blackwell, 1967.

Braginsky, B., Braginsky, D., & Ring, K. *Methods of madness.* New York: Holt Rinehart & Winston, 1969.

Clarke, R. V., & Lester, D. *Suicide: closing the exits.* New York: Springer-Verlag, 1989.

Cornish, D. B., & Clarke, R. V. *The reasoning criminal.* New York: Springer-Verlag, 1986.

Ezzat, D. H. Kuwait. In L. A. Headley (Ed.), *Suicide in Asia and the Near East.* Berkeley, CA: University of California Press, 1983.

Hillman, J. *Suicide and the soul.* New York: Harper & Row, 1964.

Lea, S. E. G. The psychology and economics of demand. *Psychological Bulletin,* 1987, 85, 441–466.

Lester, D. Suicide and life insurance. *Psychological Reports,* 1988a, 63, 920.

Lester, D. State laws on suicide and suicide rates. *Psychological Reports,* 1988b, 62, 134.

Lester, D. *Suicide as a learned behavior.* Springfield: Charles C Thomas, 1988c.

Lester, D. Rational choice theory and suicide. *Activitas Nervosa Superior,* 1988d, 30, 309–312.

Lester, D. The perception of different methods of suicide. *Journal of General Psychology,* 1988e, 115, 215–217.

Lester, D. Public health education against suicide. *Crisis,* 1989, 10, 181–183.

Menninger, K. *Man against himself.* New York: Harcourt Brace & World, 1938.

Newman, G. *Just and painful.* New York: Macmillan, 1983.

Scheff, T. *Being mentally ill.* Chicago: Aldine, 1966.

Simpson, M. E., & Conklin, G. H. Socioeconomic development, suicide and religion. *Social Forces,* 1989, 67, 945–964.

Victoroff, V. M. *The suicidal patient.* Oradell, NJ: Medical Economics Books, 1983.

Vold, G. B. *Theoretical criminology.* New York: Oxford University Press, 1979.

von Hirsch, A. *Doing justice.* New York: Hill and Wang, 1976.

Chapter 3

A POSITIVIST INDIVIDUALISTIC THEORY OF SUICIDE

The classical theory of crime reviewed in the previous chapter is one of the major *individualistic* theories of crime because it focusses on the individual criminal and how he might be deterred from engaging in criminal acts. Within a hundred years of the formulation of the classical theory of crime, people began to look at the physiological and psychological characteristics of criminals and the circumstances of their social milieu for an explanation of why people turn to criminal behavior. This *positivist* school rejected the emphasis on free will of the classical school in favor of determinism. They sought to identify the *causes* of criminal behavior using value-free scientific methods.

In this chapter, we will focus on the individualistic approaches in this positivist school, and we can identify three major thrusts in the search for an explanation of criminal behavior: physiological, psychological and psychiatric.

POSITIVIST INDIVIDUALISTIC THEORIES OF CRIME

Physiological Explanations

The first major criminologist to suggest that criminals might have different physiological characteristics was an Italian physician Cesare Lombroso (1835–1909) (Wolfgang, 1961). He felt that some individuals were "born" criminals and could be identified by their physical appearance which he thought resembled man's evolutionary ancestors. Lombroso's ideas were developed by Raffaele Garofalo (1851–1934) (Garofalo, 1968) and Enrico Ferri (1856–1929) (Sellin, 1970) and attacked by Charles Goring (1870–1919) (Goring, 1972).

Rather than reviewing the historical development of these ideas, it makes more sense to look at some modern formulations of this school of thought.

The Heredity of Crime

Some work has been done in recent years on whether there could be genetic basis for criminal behavior. One of the sound methodologies for studying whether a behavior is inherited is to compare the similarities for some target behavior of identical and non-identical twins reared together and reared apart. Christiansen (1977) reviewed the research up to that date and found that all of the studies found a higher degree of similarity (or concordance) in criminal history in identical twins than in non-identical twins. However, no study had reported on identical twins reared apart. In all of the research conducted by different investigators, Christiansen found a total of eight such pairs, with a concordance rate of 50 percent, which is lower than the composite concordance rate of 71 percent for the studies on identical twins reared together reviewed by Christiansen.

The second sound methodology for exploring the hereditability of a behavior is to look at children of parents with the target behavior who are adopted. Do they show the target behavior despite being raised by parents who do not have this behavior? Hutchings and Mednick (1977) reported on 1145 adoptees for whom the criminal history of the biological and adoptive fathers was known. The percentages of adoptees who had a criminal history for the four possibilities were:

		biological father criminal	
		yes	no
	yes	36.2%	11.5%
adoptive father criminal			
	no	22.0%	10.5%

It can be seen that the having a criminal biological father increases the chance that the son will be a criminal, whereas having a criminal adoptive father has less of an impact.

A final approach to the study of the genetics of criminal behavior has been to search for specific genetic defects that might be associated with criminal behavior. In the 1960s, interest grew in a genetic defect called the *XYY Syndrome* in which males have an extra Y sex chromosome. At first it was thought that these men had a greater tendency to become violent criminals. Indeed, the best estimates were that this syndrome was found in about 0.01 percent of newborn males, 1 percent of men in criminal or penal institutions and 2 percent of men in mental-penal institutions (Hook, 1973). However, later research threw some doubt on this association. For example, Witkin et al. (1976) located all men born in Copenhagen from 1944 to 1947. They traced 91 percent of those who were 184 centimeters tall or higher, and among these 4139 men they found twelve XYY men. Five of these men had committed crimes as compared to 9 percent of the normal men, but only one of the XYY men had committed a violent crime. Furthermore, the XYY men had lower intelligence test scores than the normal men, and this was found to be the major factor associated with their increased likelihood of committing a crime. The XYY men, however, had a higher incidence of abnormal brain electrical activity, and this might also have contributed to the increased likelihood of criminal behavior in XYY men.

Body Build and Crime

It had long been suggested that criminals differed in physique from non-criminals. In modern times, Sheldon (1949) argued that criminals were more likely to have a mesomorphic physique (with a high proportion of muscle and bone), but Sheldon's general theory of personality has fallen out of favor in recent years with psychologists. More recent research by Glueck and Glueck (1974) and Cortes and Gatti (1972) has supported the association, though other investigators have reported a failure to find any association (McCandless et al., 1972).

Biochemical Theories

Several investigators are working on biochemical causes of criminal behavior, and many of these investigations are focussing on diet. For example, delinquents have been found to behave better in institutions if placed on a diet with reduced amounts of sugar (Schoenthaler and Doraz, 1983).

Other investigators are exploring the incidence of neurological dysfunction in delinquents. For example, habitually aggressive youths are found to have an increased incidence of abnormal electrical activity in their brains (Williams, 1969), while other investigators have reported a high incidence of learning disabilities in delinquents (Murray, 1976).

Psychological Approaches

There are many psychological approaches to the study of criminal behavior, and the following is meant to be a sampling of the ideas rather than a thorough review.

Personality Traits

A great deal of research had been conducted into the personality of criminals, and intelligence (which can be viewed as a personality trait) (Heim, 1970) has received a great deal of attention. Hirschi and Hindelang (1977) reviewed the research and concluded that intelligence was a stronger predictor of delinquency than race or social class. They suggested that low intelligence increases the likelihood of criminal behavior because of its effects on school performance.

Another set of studies into the personality of criminals has been stimulated by Eysenck (1977), who argued that criminals were characterized by high levels of neuroticism and extraversion. (Eysenck believed in the physiological basis of both extraversion and neuroticism, and so his theory fits equally well into the preceding section.)

The Development of Criminal Tendencies

Several psychological theories of crime focus on childhood experiences which may facilitate the development of criminal tendencies. Freud's psychoanalytic theory postulated the existence of three subsets of wishes in the mind. The id set contains wishes which are primitive, aggressive and unorganized. Many of the id wishes first appeared in childhood and, since we were eventually punished for expressing them, have been repressed into our unconscious. The superego set of wishes are those taken in from others, especially our parents. They involve prohibitions ("Don't do that!") and ideals ("Be academically smart!"). The ego subset of wishes are compromises between our id wishes and our superego wishes, and are mature, adult and rational desires. The psychoanalytic view of one type of criminal is that he has strong id wishes which motivate behavior because the ego and superego wishes are not strong enough to inhibit them and channel them into socially acceptable desires and behaviors. This state of affairs is the result of childhood rearing patterns. Redl and Wineman (1951) suggested that parental rejection and cruelty and the absence of good parental role models play important roles here.

In contrast, social learning theory argues that criminal behavior may be learned (Bandura and Walters, 1959). Perhaps children observe their role models performing criminal behaviors. For example, child abusers often raise children who, later as parents, also become child abusers. Furthermore, if the peer group is committing criminal acts, then performance of these acts brings rewards from the peer group when you commit the same acts.

Psychiatric Approaches

The major psychiatric contribution to the understanding of criminal behavior is to view it as a psychiatric disorder or as the product of a psychiatric disorder.

One possible psychiatric diagnosis is *antisocial personality trait disturbance*, and people with this diagnosis used to be called *psychopaths* or *sociopaths* (Toch, 1979). The defining characteristic of psychopaths is that they show a chronic pattern of antisocial behavior with no shame, guilt or remorse after their actions. They tend to be free of other signs of psychiatric disturbance, to have good intelligence and to be very good at manipulating other people. There are, as you might expect, many theories of what causes psychopathy, both physiological and psychological.

A second influence of the psychiatric approach to criminal behavior has been to note that many criminals are psychiatrically disturbed with disorders other than psychopathy. Criminals are found to be suffering from psychoses, neuroses, personality disorders as well as transient situational disorders (Toch, 1979).

This has led to courts varying the sentence given to an offender, as well as the verdict, if psychiatric disorder can be demonstrated in the offender. The insanity plea defense argues that the defendant is not guilty because he or she is insane (Dreher, 1967). There are various definitions of "insanity," but a modern criterion proposed by the federal judge David Bazelon is that the accused is not responsible for his act if the act was the result of a mental disorder or mental defect (Durham v. United States, 214 F. 2d 862, 871 [1954]). In this case, the verdict is usually "not guilty through reason of insanity" or, more recently, "guilty but insane."

POSITIVIST INDIVIDUALISTIC THEORIES OF SUICIDE

The majority of the research and theorizing into the reasons why people commit suicide, of course, fall into this type of theory. This is not the place to review the many thousands of studies (see Lester [1983] for a review of recent literature), but the results can be summarized here quite briefly.

Biochemical Aspects of Suicide

A great deal of research has been conducted in recent years into the biochemical and physiological basis for suicide, and this research has been reviewed by Lester (1988a). Lester concluded that the evidence shows that suicidal involvement may be associated with abnormal responding on the dexamethasone suppression test, lower levels of 5-hydroxyindoleacetic acid in the cerebrospinal fluid, a lower nor-epinephrine/epinephrine ratio in the urine and lower levels of serotonin in the brain. Overall, the serotonergic system seems the most likely neurotransmitter involved in suicide. Lester commented that the majority of the research studies, however, have failed to control for the type and severity of psychiatric disturbance. Furthermore, the serotonergic system has been implicated in other symptoms, too, including arson, idiopathic pain, and assaultive aggression. Thus, much work remains to be done before we can draw definite conclusions about the biochemical basis for suicide.

Psychological Aspects of Suicide

There is, of course, a great deal of research into psychological concomitants and causes of suicide. Both Freudian theories (Litman, 1966) and social learning theories (Lester, 1987) have been proposed. Among the noteworthy research studies is Beck's work demonstrating the association of depression and, in particular, the cognitive component of depression (which he has called hopelessness) with suicide (Beck et al., 1975). In addition, low self-esteem has been consistently implicated as accompanying suicidal involvement (Lester, 1983).

Psychiatric Aspects of Suicide

Psychiatric research has focussed on the high incidence of psychiatric illness among suicides and the high rates of suicide in those with psychiatric diagnoses (Robins, 1981). Psychosis and substance abuse, in particular, are associated with a high incidence of suicide (Lester, 1983).

What might be of interest for this chapter, however, is to examine one specific theory of crime in detail and see what research from the suicidology literature is relevant to it.

AN EXAMPLE OF APPLYING A SPECIFIC THEORY OF CRIME TO SUICIDE

Lester (1990) has taken a theory of crime proposed by Ellis (1987a, 1987b) and explored whether it might apply to suicide. His paper will illustrate the usefulness of this approach in the search for new ideas in suicide research.

From his reviews of the research literature, Ellis identified several commonly found correlates of criminal behavior. Demographically, Ellis identified: (1) instability in the marital bonds of the person's parents, (2) a large number of siblings, (3) being black, (4) having low social status, (5) urban residence, (6) being male, and (7) being 12 to 30 years of age.

For personality-behavior, Ellis identified a further eight commonly found correlates: (1) defiance of punishment, (2) poor school performance, (3) impulsiveness and unstable work history, (4) childhood hyperactivity, (5) risk-taking and excitement-seeking behavior, (6) recreational use of drugs, (7) a preference for active and chaotic social interactions, and (8) tendencies to seek broad-ranging sexual experiences and thereby to form unstable bonds with partners.

Ellis noted that three recent theories of criminal behavior have proposed fairly specific neurological processes as causal factors. Eysenck (1977) proposed that criminals have inherited nervous systems that are unusually well "insulated" from the environmental stimuli, making them more difficult to classically condition, more tolerant of pain and more likely to be sensation seekers. A second theory has focussed on mild non-convulsive brain seizures most often provoked under conditions of stress and alcohol consumption (Mark and Ervin, 1970; Monroe, 1970). A third theory has focussed on differential hemispheric functioning in the neocortex. A good deal of research implicates holistic, intuitive and emotional thoughts in criminal behavior, processes believed to be controlled in most people by the right hemisphere.

Ellis perceived all three theories as congruent since they all describe effects of exposing the central nervous system to high levels of androgens. Ellis argued that androgens appear to lower the overall responsiveness of the brain's arousal mechanisms to stimuli, increase the probability of seizures (particularly in the limbic system), and increase the dominance of the right hemisphere.

Ellis then reviewed research which indicated that androgens (or being male) could account for many of the demographic and personality-behavioral correlates of criminality (except of course for race, number of siblings, parental bonding, urban residence, and low social status).

Ellis speculated upon the mechanism by which androgens might affect the central nervous system. He noted that exposure of the brain to high levels of testosterone or its metabolite (estradiol) during the neuro-organizational stage of brain development alters the levels of specific neurotransmitters, including the catecholamines (epinephrine, norepinephrine and dopamine) and serotonin (Heritage et al., 1980; Zuckerman, 1984). Thus, he suggested that these neurotransmitters may mediate the effect that sex hormones have on brain functioning and, therefore, on criminal behavior.

Suicidal Behavior

Is there any evidence that Ellis's theory could have some application to suicidal behavior? First let us consider the three physiological theories reviewed by Ellis.

Suicide and Eysenck's Theory of Criminality

Lester (1988a) reviewed the research into suicidal behavior and found that it was consistent with Eysenck's theory. According to Eysenck's theory, criminals are extraverted neurotics. Although research has indicated that suicidal individuals have higher levels of neuroticism than non-suicidal individuals, the research results on extraversion/introversion are inconsistent. However, impulsiveness, which is one component of extraversion, is often found to be associated with suicidal behavior.

Lester (1983) reviewed research on chronic suicide attempters and concluded that they are usually described as having a personality disorder, more often unemployed, more likely to have a criminal record, and more likely to be alcohol abusers. In these respects, chronic suicide attempters appear to be unsocialized individuals, similar in personality and behavior to criminals. However, there is, as yet, very little research, if any, on the arousability and sensitivity of the central nervous system of suicidal people.

Suicide and the Seizure Theory of Criminality

There is some evidence to support conceptualizing suicidal individuals as having seizure problems. In reviews of the research, both Barraclough (1981) and Lester (1988a) have concluded that epileptics have an increased risk of suicide, and Barraclough has concluded that the risk is especially high in those with temporal lobe epilepsy. Struve (1986) has argued that suicidal behavior is more common in those with paroxysmal electroencephalograms. In addition, Struve has reported that the suicidal behavior of those with paroxysmal EEGs is more impulsive and, for women with paroxysmal EEGs, the taking of oral contraceptives increases the likelihood of suicidal behavior. There is evidence also from Small (1970) and others that six-per-second spikes and wave complexes are associated with an increased likelihood of suicidal behavior, but the research is not altogether consistent on this point.

Suicide and the Right Hemispheric Theory of Criminality

There is little evidence relevant to whether suicidal people do or do not differ in the so-called right versus left-hemisphere thinking. Studies of thinking in suicidal individuals have not considered tasks relevant to this dimension of cognitive functioning. However, Ellis did note in passing that criminality is associated with left-handedness (at least in males) which he saw as consistent with right-hemisphere dominance. Chyatte and Smith (1981), in the only report on handedness in suicidal individuals to appear so far, found that Navy recruits who made mild suicide attempts were more likely to be left-handed than expected. The left-handed attempters were more likely to abuse alcohol than were the right-handed attempters.

Androgens and Suicide

Most of the research on the sex hormones and suicide has focussed on the fact that the rate of attempted suicide in women has been found to vary consistently over the menstrual cycle, being higher during the premenstrual and bleeding phases (Lester, 1984). Indeed, it has been suggested that estrogens may play a direct role in the higher rates of attempted suicide in women than in men.

In contrast, very little research has focussed on the levels of androgrens in suicides. In the only study so far to report on testosterone levels in suicidal men, Roland et al. (1986) found higher levels of serum testosterone in male completed suicides than in men dying suddenly from other causes.

Neurotransmitters and Suicide

As mentioned earlier in this chapter, the serotonergic system seems the most likely neurotransmitter system involved in suicide. Since serotonin has figured in the major biochemical theories of depression, the research on suicides fits nicely since the majority of suicides are depressed.

However, other possibilities have been proposed; that serotonin may be related to the impulsivity of suicidal behavior or that serotonin may affect the violence of the suicide attempt (Lester, 1988a).

Demographic Characteristics

Of the seven demographic traits listed by Ellis as characteristic of criminals, research into the demographic correlates of suicide have shown that parental discord is clearly associated with an increased likelihood of suicide. Jacobs (1971) has documented the effect of broken marriages on the suicidal behavior of adolescents, and Phillips (1979), in a review of the literature, has found a high incidence of loss of parents due to divorce or separation (but not death) in the childhoods of suicidal people.

Males have higher rates of completed suicide, while females have higher rates of attempted suicide in the USA and in almost all countries of the world (Lester, 1984). In contrast, being black is associated with a *lesser* risk of suicide (Lester, 1972).

Suicide rates increase with age for males in the USA and peak in middle age for females in the USA. However, this pattern is not found in all countries (Lester, 1982), although, except in the poorest countries, suicide rates are generally lower in the youth. In recent years, the suicide rates of youths have been increasing in many countries, including the

USA, so that their suicide rates are now quite high, especially in the USA for white males (Lester, 1988b). Thus, especially nowadays, completed suicide does increase dramatically in frequency at puberty and is one of the leading causes of death in youth.

Urban residence is often found to be associated with an increased suicidal risk, though this relationship is not always found (Lester, 1972, 1983). Higher urban suicide rates were reported in the 1970s in Alabama, England, Singapore, and Sweden, while higher rural rates have been reported in Greece, Rhode Island, the state of Delhi (India), Japan and Rhodesia (Lester, 1983). However, research before the 1970s generally reported higher urban rates, for example, in the USA, Ceylon and Hong Kong (Lester, 1972). Much more research is required to ascertain under what conditions a higher urban rate of completed suicide is found.

Social class has not received much attention from suicidologists. Maris (1967) found that completed suicide in Chicago was more common in the lower classes. However, in England, Stengel (1964) claimed that completed suicide was more common in the upper classes, except for those aged 65 and older when the rate was higher in the lower classes.

Research in the USA has focussed on suicide rates in specific occupational groups, and rates of completed suicide have been reported as higher in those with lower occupational status (for example, Tuckman et al., 1964).

Finally, the number of siblings has not received special attention from suicidologists. Occasionally, incidental data are reported. Lester (1972, 1983) found three studies reporting no difference between the sibship size of attempted suicides and controls, one study reporting larger sibships and one study reporting smaller sibships. For completed suicides, two studies reported no differences. However, the samples in these studies were quite small, and no study based on adequate samples has yet appeared.

Conclusions

We can conclude from this review of research into suicide on demographic characteristics that unstable parental marriages and being male are clearly associated with an increased likelihood of *completed* suicide. Unstable parental marriages and being female are associated with an increased likelihood of *attempted* suicide. Race is also clearly associated with suicidal behavior, with blacks having a lower rate of completed suicide.

Thus, it may be argued that gender affects the type of suicidal behavior chosen. Ellis argued that gender is related to the incidence of crime, but others have noted that the type of antisocial acts chosen by female youths are different from those chosen by male youths. Ellis is correct in noting that male youths are more likely to commit crimes against people and property, but female youths are more likely to choose self-destructive ways of acting out, such as running away from home or being sexually promiscuous. So perhaps, just as gender affects the type of antisocial behavior chosen, gender may also affect the type of suicidal behavior chosen.

The effect of race may be similar here. Blacks may choose different ways of reacting to frustration and stress than whites, with assaultive behavior more common in blacks and suicidal behavior more common in whites.

Ellis's theory when applied to suicide points to areas of research that have been relatively neglected (especially as compared to research conducted on crime and delinquency). Very little attention has been paid by suicidologists to number of siblings, social class and urban/rural residence. Ellis's theory may be heuristic in this regard in stimulating suicidologists to study these variables more extensively in the future.

Personality-Behavioral Characteristics

Of the eight personality-behavioral traits proposed by Ellis as common in delinquents and criminals, several are also well documented in suicidal individuals. For example, Platt (1984, 1986) has reviewed research which indicates that unemployment is clearly more common in both male attempted and completed suicides, though an unstable work history aside from unemployment has not been studied.

Impulsivity has been found to be common in attempted suicides, especially in youth (Kessel, 1967; Corder et al., 1974). There is also some evidence that attempted suicides are risk-takers. For example, they gamble more money in laboratory situations (Adams et al., 1973) and engage in more risky behaviors such as reckless driving and alcohol misuse (Steiner, 1972). However, such differences are not always reported (Kochansky, 1973).

Surprisingly, very little research has been conducted on the academic performance of suicides. Related to this variable, while Peck and Schrut (1971) found that college students in general in the USA had an average rate of suicide, Kitagawa and Hauser (1973) reported that the least educated males in the USA completed suicide at twice the rate of the best educated males, and Li (1972) reported the same phenomenon in Taiwan.

Although substance abuse is associated with higher rates of both attempted and completed suicide (Lester, 1972, 1983), the study of *recreational* drug use in suicides has not been studied. Neither is there any research on defiance of punishment, seeking a broad range of sexual experiences, and a preference for chaotic social interactions.

Conclusions

As with our review of demographic variables, this review of research on suicidal individuals into the personality-behavioral variables proposed by Ellis as characteristic of criminals reveals support for some variables and a lack of research for others.

Suicidal people are often impulsive, may be risk-takers, and do have higher rates of unemployment. However, much more research needs to be conducted on suicidal people to explore the relevance for suicide of the other characteristics proposed by Ellis.

Discussion

The present section has shown that Ellis's theory of criminality may have usefulness for the understanding of suicidal behavior. At the present time, it is difficult to assess whether the theory will fit completed suicide or attempted suicide better.

The most striking finding when the research on suicide is examined for the presence or absence of characteristics proposed by Ellis is that little or no research exists for many of the characteristics. It appears, therefore, that characteristics which have intrigued criminologists have not occurred to suicidologists as worthy of study. This analysis of the applicability of Ellis's theory to suicide, therefore, may have most impact in urging suicidologists to explore the relevance of such characteristics.

For example, until the 1980s, no research study on suicide had ever looked at handedness or testosterone levels. In the 1980s, so far, only one study has appeared on each of these variables. Very little research has appeared on intelligence and school performance of suicidal youth, whereas these variables have been thoroughly explored by criminologists.

IMPLICATIONS FOR PREVENTING SUICIDE

The positivist individualistic approach to understanding suicide has dominated the prevention scene for several decades now. Three major prevention techniques have developed from this approach.

Psychiatric Treatment

Since suicide is associated with psychiatric disorder, treatment of the underlying psychiatric disorder with the appropriate medications (and perhaps electroconvulsive therapy) should reduce the risk of suicide. Barraclough (1972), for example, looked at one hundred suicides and judged that forty-four had previous depressive episodes, of whom twenty-one met the criteria for recurrent affective illness. He argued that treatment with lithium would have saved many of those lives.

Since the medications used to treat psychiatric disorders can often be used for committing suicide, consideration is now being given to the toxicity of medications, and physicians are being urged to prescribe those medications which are less often used for suicide (Henry, 1988).

Psychotherapy

Psychotherapy is also a major treatment recommendation for suicidal people. Various therapeutic strategies have been used. Liberman and Eckman (1981) argued for the usefulness of behavior therapy, while others (for example, Patsiokas and Clum, 1985) have argued for the usefulness of cognitive therapy.

Crisis Intervention

Since 1950, a large number of suicide prevention and crisis intervention centers have been opened. These typically use paraprofessionals to respond to suicidal individuals over the telephone, using client-centered therapy to explore the feelings of the caller, followed for some crisis services by efforts to find immediate solutions for some of the problems which the caller is confronting (Lester and Brockopp, 1973).

In addition to these services, a growing number of self-help groups for those who have survived the suicide of a loved one have been established, both to help the survivors come to terms with the suicide and to prevent them from subsequently committing suicide (Lukas and Seiden, 1987).

Despite the predominance of these prevention techniques, we mentioned in the introduction that the suicide rate of the USA has remained quite steady in recent years. Thus, these techniques do not appear to be having any impact on suicidal behavior. Perhaps one reason for these is that they are passive techniques. The psychiatrist, psychotherapist, or crisis intervention worker has to wait for a suicidal crisis to develop in an individual and for that individual to contact them for help. It may be that potential suicides do not seek help in sufficient numbers for treatment to have an impact on the suicide rate.

Furthermore, these techniques are secondary and tertiary prevention which are concerned with preventing the reoccurrence of suicide in those who have already attempted suicide and intervention with those on the brink of suicide. This may be too late. Primary prevention, prevention of the development of suicidal tendencies, would be expected to have a greater impact on the prevention of suicide, but primary prevention techniques have not yet been proposed, let alone tried out (Lester, 1988c).

REFERENCES

Adams, R., Giffen, M., & Garfield, F. Risk taking among suicide attempters. *Journal of Abnormal Psychology,* 1973, 82, 262–267.

Bandura, A., & Walters, R. *Adolescent aggression.* New York: Ronald, 1959.

Barraclough, B. M. Suicide prevention, recurrent affective disorder and lithium. *British Journal of Psychiatry,* 1972, 121, 391–392.

Barraclough, B. M. Suicide and epilepsy. In E. H. Reynolds & M. R. Trimble (Eds.), *Epilepsy and psychiatry.* Edinburgh: Churchill Livingston, 1981, pp. 72–77.

Beck, A. T., Kovacs, M., & Weissman, A. Hopelessness and suicidal behavior. *Journal of the American Medical Association,* 1975, 234, 1146–1149.

Christiansen, K. O. A review of studies of criminality among twins. In S. A. Mednick & K. O. Christiansen (Eds.), *Biosocial bases of criminal behavior.* New York: Gardner, pp. 45–88.

Chyatte, C., & Smith, V. Brain asymmetry predicts suicide among Navy alcohol abusers. *Military Medicine,* 1981, 146, 277–278.

Corder, B., Shorr, W., & Corder, R. A study of social and psychological characteristics of adolescent suicide attempters in an urban disadvantaged area. *Adolescence,* 1974, 9, 1–6.

Cortes, J. B., & Gatti, F. M. *Delinquency and crime.* New York: Seminar, 1972.

Dreher, R. H. Origin, development, and present status of insanity as a defense to criminal responsibility in the common law. *Journal of the History of the Behavioral Sciences,* 1967, 3, 47–57.

Ellis, L. Relationships of criminality and psychopathy with eight other apparent behavioral manifestations of sub-optimal arousal. *Personality & Individual Differences,* 1987a, 8, 905–925.

Ellis, L. Neurohormonal bases of varying tendencies to learn delinquent and criminal behavior. In E. K. Morris & C. J. Braukman (Eds.), *Behavioral approaches to crime and delinquency*. New York: Plenum, 1987b, pp. 499–518.

Eysenck, H. J. *Crime and personality*. London: Routledge & Kegan Paul, 1977.

Garofalo, R. *Criminology*. Translated by R. Miller. Montclair, NJ: Patterson Smith, 1968.

Glueck, S., & Glueck, E. *Of delinquency and crime*. Springfield, IL: Charles C Thomas, 1974.

Goring, C. *The English convict*. Montclair, NJ: Patterson Smith, 1970.

Heim, A. W. *Intelligence and personality*. Harmondsworth: Penguin, 1970.

Henry, J. A. Toxicity in overdose. In B. E. Leonard & S. W. Parker (Eds.), *Current approaches: risks/benefits of antidepressants*. Southampton, UK: Duphar Laboratories, 1988, pp. 44–52.

Heritage, A. S., Stumpf, W. E. Sar, M., & Grant, L. D. Brainstem catecholamine neurons are target sites for sex steroid hormones. *Science*, 1980, 207, 1377–1379.

Hirschi, T., & Hindelang, M. Intelligence and delinquency. *American Sociological Review*, 1977, 42, 471–586.

Hook, E. Behavioral implications of the human XYY genotype. *Science*, 1973, 179, 139–150.

Hutchings, B., & Mednick, S. A. Criminality in adoptees and their adoptive and biological parents. In S. A. Mednick & K. O. Christiansen (Eds.), *Biosocial bases of criminal behavior*. New York: Gardner, 1977, pp. 127–141.

Jacobs, J. *Adolescent suicide*. New York: Wiley, 1971.

Kessel, N. Self-poisoning. In E. S. Shneidman (Ed.), *Essays in self-destruction*. New York: Science House, 1967, pp. 345–372.

Kitagawa, E., & Hauser, P. *Differential mortality in the United States*. Cambridge: Harvard University Press, 1973.

Kochansky, G. Risk-taking and hedonic mood stimulation in suicide attempters. *Journal of Abnormal Psychology*, 1973, 81, 80–86.

Lester, D. *Why people kill themselves*, 1st Ed. Springfield, IL: Charles C Thomas, 1972.

Lester, D. The distribution of sex and age among completed suicide. *International Journal of Social Psychiatry*, 1982, 28, 256–260.

Lester, D. *Why people kill themselves*, 2nd Ed. Springfield, IL: Charles C Thomas, 1983.

Lester, D. Suicide. In C. S. Widom (Ed.), *Sex roles and psychopathology*. New York: Plenum, 1984, pp. 145–156.

Lester, D. *Suicide as a learned behavior*. Springfield, IL: Charles C Thomas, 1987.

Lester, D. *The biochemical basis of suicide*. Springfield, IL: Charles C Thomas, 1988a.

Lester, D. Youth suicide. *Adolescence*, 1988b, 23, 955–958.

Lester, D. Preventing suicide. In M. A. Morgan & J. D. Morgan (Eds.), *Thanatology*. London, Ont: King's College, 1988c, pp. 427–437.

Lester, D. The relevance of Ellis's neurohormonal theory of crime and delinquency to suicide. *Personality & Individual Differences*, 1990, in press.

Lester, D., & Brockopp, G. W. *Crisis intervention and counseling by telephone.* Springfield, IL: Charles C Thomas, 1973.

Li, W. Suicide and educational attainment in a transitional society. *Sociological Quarterly,* 1972, 13, 253–258.

Liberman, R., & Eckman, T. Behavior therapy versus insight-oriented therapy for repeated suicide attempters. *Archives of General Psychiatry,* 1981, 38, 1126–1130.

Litman, R. E. Sigmund Freud on suicide. *Psychoanalytic Forum,* 1966, 1, 206–214.

Lukas, C., & Seiden, H. M. *Silent grief.* New York: Scribners, 1987.

Maris, R. Suicide, status and mobility in Chicago. *Social Forces,* 1967, 46, 246–256.

Mark, V. H., & Ervin, F. R. *Violence and the brain.* New York: Harper & Row, 1970.

McCandless, B. R., Persons, W. S., & Roberts, A. Perceived opportunity, delinquency, race and body build among delinquent youth. *Journal of Consulting & Clinical Psychology,* 1972, 38, 281–283.

Monroe, R. *Episodic behavioral disorder.* Cambridge: Harvard University Press, 1970.

Murray, C. *The link between learning disabilities and juvenile delinquency.* Washington, DC: US Government Printing Office, 1976.

Patsiokas, A. T., & Clum, G. A. Effects of psychotherapeutic strategies in the treatment of suicide attempters. *Psychotherapy,* 1985, 22, 281–290.

Peck, M., & Schrut, A. Suicidal behavior among college students. *HSMHA Health Reports,* 1971, 86, 149–171.

Phillips, D. A review of incidence of parental absence upon suicidal behavior. *Proceedings of the 9th International Congress for Suicide Prevention.* Ottawa: IASP, 1979, pp. 50–53.

Platt, S. Unemployment and suicidal behavior. *Social Science & Medicine,* 1984, 19, 93–115.

Platt, S. Parasuicide and unemployment. *British Journal of Psychiatry,* 1986, 149, 401–405.

Redl, F., & Wineman, D. *Children who hate.* New York: Free Press, 1951.

Robins, E. *The final months.* New York: Oxford University Press, 1981.

Roland, B. C., Morris, J. L., & Zelhart, P. F. Proposed relation of testosterone levels to male suicides and sudden deaths. *Psychological Reports,* 1986, 59, 100–102.

Schoenthaler, S., & Doraz, W. Diet and crime. *International Journal of Biosocial Research,* 1983, 4, 29–39.

Sellin, T. Enrico Ferri. In H. Mannheim (Ed.), *Pioneers in criminology.* Montclair, NJ: Patterson Smith, 1970, pp. 232–271.

Sheldon, W. H. *Varieties of delinquent youth.* New York: Harper, 1949.

Small, J. Small sharp spikes in a psychiatric population. *Archives of General Psychiatry,* 1970, 22, 277–284.

Steiner, J. A questionnaire study of risk-taking in psychiatric patients. *British Journal of Medical Psychology,* 1972, 45, 365–374.

Stengel, E. *Suicide and attempted suicide.* Baltimore: Penguin, 1964.

Struve, F. Clinical electroencephalography and the study of suicidal behavior. *Suicide & Life-Threatening Behavior,* 1986, 16, 133–165.

Toch, H. *Psychology of crime and criminal justice.* New York: Holt, Rinehart & Winston, 1979.

Tuckman, J., Youngman, W. F., & Kreizman, G. Occupation and suicide. *Industrial Medicine & Surgery,* 1964, 33, 818–820.

Williams, D. Neural factors related to habitual aggression. *Brain,* 1969, 92, 503–520.

Witkin, H., Mednick, S., Schulsinger, F., Bakkestrom, E., Christiansen, K., Goodenough, D., Hirschhorn, K., Lundsteen, C., Owen, D., Philip, J., Rubin, D., & Stocking, M. Criminality in XYY and XXY men. *Science,* 1976, 193, 547–555.

Wolfgang, M. E. Pioneers in criminology: Cesare Lombroso. *Journal of Criminal Law, Criminology, & Police Science,* 1961, 52, 361–369.

Zuckerman, M. Sensation seeking. *Behavioral & Brain Sciences,* 1984, 7, 413–471.

Chapter 4

A SOCIAL STRUCTURE THEORY OF SUICIDE

There are several positivist theories of crime which focus on the social structure or organization of society as causative factors. Some of these theories focus on the destructive social forces which arise from the prevailing cultural norms and values existing in lower-class culture and may be called *culture deviance theories,* while another set focusses upon the frustration felt by lower-class youths when they are prevented from obtaining rewards in the legitimate sphere and may be called *strain theories.*

Culture Deviance Theory

If the cultural values of the people in the area you grow up in do not conform to those of the main society, then conformity to these deviant rules, values and norms will lead to deviant behavior.

Shaw and McKay

Shaw and McKay (1972), studying Chicago in the 1920s, noted that the city had greatly differing neighborhoods. Some were marked by wealth and luxury while others were slums. Shaw and McKay argued that delinquency was caused by the conditions in these slum areas. Often, teenage gangs developed in these neighborhoods, and these gangs assisted the youths to survive and provided economic gain and friendship. The gangs then served as cultural agents, transmitting the new norms and values to the younger kids as they grew up and joined the gangs.

Shaw and McKay documented differences in attitudes and values in the different neighborhoods in Chicago and different patterns of child rearing. Parents in the neighborhoods with low crime rates stressed the importance of school, church and other community organizations, and families were tightly knit. In the neighborhoods with high crime rates, there was a conflict in the cultural values, rather than a homogeneous deviant culture. Some families continued to stress conventional values,

44

while others rejected such values. The youths in these neighborhoods had to choose with which set of values to align themselves, and they often chose the deviant set of values.

Walter Miller

Miller (1958) also explained crime and delinquency as a the result of lower-class culture. He stressed the role of female-headed households with the absence of good male role models for the adolescents, and he felt that the absence of men facilitated the establishment of male gangs as a substitute. He also noted the importance of several focal concerns in this culture which become goals: getting into and staying out of trouble, recognition of physical and mental toughness, establishing an image of street-wise smartness, the search for excitement, a belief in fate and luck as determinants of outcomes in life, and a concern with personal freedom and autonomy. Youths who become delinquents and criminals do so by conforming to these cultural demands.

Thorsten Sellin

Sellin (1938) stressed the role of conflict in norms. He argued that every individual knows the right and wrong way to behave in situations. In the normal process of growing up and becoming socialized, these norms clash, leading to culture conflict. Primary conflict occurs when two different cultures conflict, while secondary conflict occurs within the development of a single culture. An immigrant to the USA who behaves according to the norms of his home country illustrates primary conflict. A conflict between the values of native-born lower-class youths and middle-class values illustrates secondary conflict, and it this type of conflict that is responsible for a high rate of crime.

Wolfgang and Ferracuti

Wolfgang and Ferracuti (1967) proposed a subcultural theory of crime which suggested that there was a subculture which had its own norms separate from those of the dominant culture. In particular, Wolfgang and Ferracuti suggested that a common subculture was one of violence, especially among some groups of the population (such as younger men) and in some regions, such as the southern states of America (Lester, 1986–1987).

Strain Theory

Strain theories focus on the feelings of the those in different groups or subcultures in the society. If you are unable to achieve success, prestige or status through legitimate means, then it is likely that you will feel anger and frustration. Strain theories propose that we all share similar goals and values (a very different assumption from the cultural deviance theories), but that we differ in our ability to achieve these goals, especially if we come from the lower social classes.

Robert Merton

Merton (1957) argued that social structures establish goals for the members of the society and label some methods for obtaining these goals as approved. Non-conforming behavior results when people reject either the goals or the means for obtaining the goals. Merton suggested that modern America emphasizes goals rather than means and that the most sought-after goal is wealth and material goods.

He identified five methods or *modes* of adaptation available to members of society. *Conformists* accept both the goals and the approved means to obtain them. *Innovators* accept the goals but reject the approved means, as when a youth steals a car. *Ritualists* reject the goals but accept the approved means and, therefore, go through the rituals without any fundamental commitment to the goals toward which they appear to be aiming. *Retreatists* reject both the goals and the approved means and are illustrated by psychotics, vagabonds and vagrants. *Rebels* not only reject both the goals and the approved means, but they set out to establish a new social order. It can be seen that criminals fall mainly into the innovator type.

Albert Cohen

Cohen (1955) argued that the criminal behavior in slum districts is really a protest against the norms and values of middle-class culture. The social conditions of the slums make it difficult, if not impossible, for the youths to obtain the approved goals by the approved methods. These youths experience frustration which results in non-utilitarian, malicious and negativistic behavior. Parents in these districts fail to teach their children the proper skills for entering into the middle-class culture, and so their children lack educational and communication skills and are unable to delay gratification. They fail to measure up to the *middle-class measuring rods.*

There are three adaptational styles which result from this failure. The *college boy* does not give up but embraces the middle-class values and tries to be successful according to these values. The *stable corner-boy* hangs out in the neighborhood, gambles, is truant from school, engages in athletics and eventually gets a menial job. He withdraws into the comfortable world of the lower class. The *delinquent boy* adapts by becoming a criminal.

Richard Cloward and Lloyd Ohlin

Cloward and Ohlin (1960) added to these analyses by noting that not even illegitimate means for achieving goals are evenly distributed in the society. Some lower-class neighborhoods provide more opportunities for getting into a criminal career. Youths who know adults already engaged in crime can enter the criminal subculture as apprentices. If the peer groups and the adults do not provide this criminal learning experience, then the youth may retreat into drug use or simply seek catharsis through violence.

Preventing Crime

This perspective on crime suggests that primary prevention could be achieved by organizing the local community. Deteriorating neighborhoods need to be improved. Shaw started the Chicago Area Project in the 1930s which aimed to set up neighborhood organizations which would strengthen controls over behavior and provide good adult role models for the youths (Kobrin, 1959). Resident involvement and responsibility were stressed, and the groups set up recreational programs, programs to improve the community, and programs to help supervise already delinquent youths.

The Mobilization for Youth Project in New York City in the 1960s sought to increase access to job opportunities for youths through education and training and to get neighborhood residents involved in community improvement and activism (Brager and Purcell, 1967). Like the Chicago Area Project, community residents ran the programs. Recreational and sports programs were established, relationships between the parents and schools developed, and job training and vocational guidance services set up. An Urban Youth Service Corps for teenagers was organized to work on neighborhood-improvement projects such as building playgrounds.

In Boston's Mid-City Project, detached street workers established contact with delinquents and gang members on their own turf and tried to help them get educational opportunities and legitimate employment, acting as go-betweens for the youths in their dealings with the criminal justice system, the school system and employers (Miller, 1962).

Social Structure Theories of Suicide: Culture Deviance Theories

Some subcultural theories have focussed on whole regions of the United States, such as the theory that there is a southern subculture (Gastil, 1971), while others have focussed on a whole social group such as the lower social class. However, subcultural theories of delinquency often focus on smaller groups, such as the gang (Cohen, 1955).

To apply subcultural theory to suicidal behavior may further reduce the size of the group involved. Groups of depressed and suicidal teenagers, for example, are often quite small. However, such groups do share values and attitudes that are common to other teenagers, and the subculture can be seen as quite large if we focus on those who hold similar attitudes and values, even if they are not in contact (as in a gang).

Lester (1987a) described the case of five teenagers of whom three killed themselves. He detailed their dependence upon a leader and the other members of the group, heavy drug involvement, preference for heavy-metal music, difficult relations with their parents characterized by intense resentment or apparent indifference, poor self-image (feelings of worthlessness and ugliness combined with shyness), and suicidal preoccupation.

Although this group was quite self-contained, their deaths generated a great deal of suicidal preoccupation and acting out in their peers. This suggests that the subcultural values were quite widespread. Interestingly, hostility was also aroused. One girl overdosed on Tylenol and, on her return to school, found a full bottle of Tylenol in her locker with a note saying, "Do it right next time."

The five teenagers formed a peer group. However, the fact that their behaviors tapped into a suicidal vein among other students in the high school points to the existence of a "peer culture" that transcended the peer group. Within each peer group, competition for status frequently occurs, which leads to experimentation with new behaviors. Thus, behaviors within a peer group (and, therefore, the peer culture) tend to become more extreme. In a suicidal subculture, overt suicidal acts seem inevitable. The existence of large numbers of peer groups within the peer subculture and the experimenting by peer groups with new behaviors indicates that the subculture is dynamic over time and is continually being modified. Thus, the teenage suicidal subculture in the next decade may be significantly different from the present subculture.

Subculture is a useful concept since it shapes our awareness of the values and attitudes that accompany participation in a particular type of behavior and draws our attention to the social shaping of behavior that can take place which, in turn, facilitates entry of people into the subculture.

Cultural Patterns and Suicide

Lester (1988) noted that Durkheim's (1897) theory of suicide has been used to predict a variety of associations between suicide rates and social indicators. For example, societies with large numbers of migrants appear likely to have lower degrees of social integration than societies with more stable populations. Similarly, societies with high rates of divorce appear likely to have lower degrees of social integration, and so higher suicide rates. Stack (1980a, 1980b) has confirmed that states in the USA with higher rates of interstate migration and higher rates of divorce do indeed have higher rates of suicide. Lester (1987b) looked at a measure of religiosity (church attendance) and found a strong association between church attendance and suicide rates in the states.

Studies of this type typically use multiple-regression analyses which select first the most powerful correlate of the suicide rate. For example, let us assume that Social Indicator A correlates with Pearson $r = 0.80$ and Social Indicator B correlates with $r = 0.81$ with the suicide rate. Although these two correlation coefficients are not significantly different, the multiple-regression analysis selects Social Indicator A as the primary correlate. Social Indicator B may not appear in the final multiple regression.

A factor analysis, on the other hand, groups all of the variables having strong intercorrelations together and permits an examination of how many clusters of social indicators exist and the extent to which they correlate with the target variables, in this case the suicide rate. Lester (1988) undertook to explore how social indicators relate to rates of suicide using factor analysis of data for the continental states of the USA in 1980. The social indicators were factor-analyzed, and seven independent factors identified. The factor scores for each factor were correlated with the states' suicide rates.

Suicide rates were significantly correlated with two factors. One appeared to measure social instability (with high loadings from the divorce rate, interstate migration and church attendance), while the other appeared to measure an east-west/conservative dimension (with high loadings from the birth rate, a high vote for Reagan as President in 1980, and longitude). It seems inappropriate to select one of the social indicators as the most critical for suicide, since states with high divorce rates also had the highest rates of interstate migration (Pearson $r = 0.74$) and both correlated strongly with the suicide rate ($r = 0.78$ for the divorce rate and 0.80 for interstate migration, correlations which are not significantly different from each other).

Lester suggested that a useful way of conceptualizing the pattern of correlations between the rate of suicide and social indicators is to see the states of the USA as having different cultural patterns. To pick out one of the components of a pattern as supporting a particular hypothesis from theory and as the most important variable in predicting suicide rates obscures the fact that these components are related and are part of a broader cultural pattern.

Subcultural Theories of the Methods Chosen for Suicide

Marks and Stokes (1976) found that southern college students had more childhood experience with guns than non-southern students. They suggested that socialization with weapons may affect choice of method for suicide. Marks and Abernathy (1974) found that the more southern a region of the USA was, the higher the proportion of suicides who used guns for killing themselves.

Lester (1986–1987) pursued this idea and showed that Gastil's (1971) index of the "southernness" of each state, while not associated with the total suicide rate of the state, was associated positively with suicide rate using firearms and negatively with the suicide rate using hanging/strangulation.

Thus, it appears useful to view a southern subculture as accounting in part for the heavy involvement of guns as a method for suicide in some regions of the USA.

Platt's Subcultural Theory

Researchers in Edinburgh, Scotland, have closely monitored attempts at suicide for over twenty years. Their data have enabled them to mark changes in the rate of attempted suicide over the years, as well as other epidemiological changes, and in addition to calculate the rates for each city ward.

For example, Platt et al. (1988) have reported attempted suicide rates for 1983–1984 of 72 per 100,000 per year for those of Social Classes I and II, 236 for those of Social Class III, 526 for those of Social Class IV, and 879 for those of Social Class V.

Platt (1985) has looked at the stable yet differing rates of attempted suicide in the city wards and formulated a subcultural hypothesis to account for them. Kreitman et al. (1970) suggested that many attempted suicides come from a group who view self-aggression as an acceptable means of conveying certain kinds of information to others. Attempted suicide is viewed as understandable and appropriate in some circumstances, if not formally condoned. Platt suggested a more formal hypothesis: there is a subculture in contemporary society in which the communicational functions of attempted suicide are particularly well-defined (Platt, 1985, p. 258).

In order to explore this idea empirically, Platt interviewed people in four areas: one with a high rate of attempted suicide (566 per 100,000 per year) and three with a low rate of attempted suicide (rates of 125, 168 and 205). He interviewed both attempted suicides and a random sample of residents in each area.

As expected, people interviewed from the area with a high rate of attempted suicide were less educated, more often from the lower social class and more likely to be renting housing rather than owning it. However, Platt found only limited evidence for different subcultural values on inventories of value orientation and evaluation of ways of behaving. Those living in the region with a high rate of attempted suicide did feel that children were more likely to leave school at age sixteen, for example, that people were more likely to have sex before marriage, that people were more likely to attempt suicide, that married couples were more likely to quarrel and row, and that men were more likely to fight in the street. However, Platt found that attempted suicide was equally and strongly proscribed in both types of regions.

Lifetime contact with suicidal behavior was extensive and similar in both types of regions, but those in the high-rate area did report more intimate and personal experience with suicidal behavior. Platt found no evidence for a *contra* culture in the region with a high rate of attempted suicide. Rather, he concluded that the people in the two types of regions differed in degree but not in kind. Although he remained convinced that a subcultural theory was useful in explaining geographical variation in rates of attempted suicide, he was aware that he had not convincingly demonstrated two distinct subcultures which would explain the differing rates of attempted suicide.

A different type of analysis comes from the work of Philip and McCulloch (1966), Morgan et al. (1975) and others. These investigators have calculated rates of attempted suicide by ward within a city and explored social correlates of these rates. For example, Philip and McCulloch found that rates of attempted suicide correlated with the incidence of juvenile delinquency, children taken into care and cases of child cruelty, and overcrowding. These studies identify sociological correlates of attempted suicide and begin to suggest components of the subculture that may be associated with high rates.

Discussion

It was suggested that the concept of a subculture may have usefulness in accounting for clusters of suicides in peer groups, especially amongst teenagers, and in explaining regional variations in the choice of methods for suicide. In addition, the possible existence of broad cultural patterns of social indicators that may be associated with suicide rates was illustrated. These illustrations suggest that cultural deviance theory of suicide can be plausibly proposed and might account for some of the phenomena observed by suicidologists.

Social Structure Theories of Suicide: Strain Theories

A strain theory approach to suicide has less previous research and theorizing to build upon than the culture deviance theories proposed above. Strain theory must focus upon the emotional experiences (such as anger and frustration) of the suicidal individual resulting from the difficulties in working toward culturally approved goals by socially acceptable means.

To some extent, suicides (or at least some types of suicides) may fit into the retreatist categories in the typologies developed by Merton and, more closely, Cloward and Ohlin. The retreatist described by Cloward and Ohlin remains loyal to the values and rules of the larger conventional society but may be incapable of following the rules successfully. After failure, they retreat from the world. Cloward and Ohlin's retreatist often takes drugs, but the suicide seeks a different form of existence: none rather than drugged. Merton's retreatist rejects both the goals and the means set up by conventional society, becomes asocialized, and is represented by the psychotic, outcasts, tramp, chronic drunkard, drug addict, vagrant and vagabond.

Suicidal individuals have failed at the tasks which others complete or, having failed, they react with much more extreme depression and despair than the rest of the population. Their response is not to continue the struggle but to withdraw from the struggle by seeking death. Having been conformists, in the midst of their crisis they become retreatists. They are, in fact, *episodic retreatists*.

A common theme in suicides is the notion that the person has failed in some way. For example, Livermore (1985) found that 30 percent of the suicide notes of those who killed themselves said "You'll be better off without me," while 5 percent of the notes from those who killed themselves and 30 percent of the notes from those who attempted suicide said "I'm a failure." In addition, Livermore noted that about half of the notes from completed suicides mentioned financial problems as one of the precipitating causes of their suicide as did a quarter of the notes from suicide attempters, suggesting that the conventional American goal of wealth was of concern to these suicidal individuals.

The small group of suicidal teenagers studied by Lester (1987a), and mentioned above, showed a heavy involvement with drugs, a fascination with heavy-metal music, poor relationships with parents, and extremely low self-esteem, values which might well characterize the retreatist life-style.

Stephens (1988), in her discussion of the suicidal behavior of women she had studied, concluded that the women "had interpersonal histories of relentlessly negative relationships (with others). . . . Their social and psychological experiences have prepared them to be victims, victims of parents, of men, of relationships in which the self is continually mortified . . . (p. 84)." These women often said that they were "bad," and they were convinced that they were different from others. Yet they desired to be normal. As one women expressed it, "All my life I've felt like nothing, nothing, just nothing." Again, these lives suggest that the women have struggled and considered themselves to have failed, and the suicidal behavior appears to be a retreatist strategy.

These ideas suggest that it would be fruitful to explore the degree to which suicidal people had and still have the conventional goals of people in their society, which methods they have tried to achieve these goals, and whether they have in fact given up trying to achieve them.

Implications for Suicide Prevention

The prevention programs stemming from the social structure perspective on crime involved primary prevention strategies, changing the community so as to make criminal behavior less likely to arise. In addition, tertiary prevention, working with delinquents to prevent future criminal behavior, was also emphasized.

Since suicide is much rarer than criminal behavior, only a few individuals in any community are suicidal or potential suicides. Even when a cluster of suicides occurs in one school, the cluster typically involves only two or three suicides. However, if we include those who are depressed, the proportion of the group included is much greater. For example, Lester (1990) found that 18 percent of a sample of high school students were considerably depressed on an objective self-report inventory as compared to only 4 percent of a sample of college students.

Primary prevention programs are more suitably set up in communities where suicide is common or likely to be, such as schools, native American reservations, and retirement communities.

What kinds of programs might be set up in schools, say, which would modify the general environment and which might prevent suicide as well? Typically, schools set up suicide awareness programs or suicide prevention programs (Rainer, 1989), but these have too narrow a focus for the social structure perspective. However, occasional school suicide prevention programs do have a broader set of goals. For example, Patrick (1989) urged: (1) efforts to create a school climate in which each and every student has opportunities to be successful and to feel valued and affirmed and in which students feel comfortable accessing help for personal issues, (2) teaching methodologies such as mastery learning and cooperative team learning that promote success, (3) positive youth development activities, (4) mentor/peer programs, and (5) developmental guidance, a health curriculum and parent education programs.

Such goals seem fine, but they appear too unfocussed to be dealing specifically with the problem of suicide. However, perhaps suicide is only one strategy that can be adopted by those who are considering or trying a retreatist strategy. Thus, it is not perhaps necessary to focus such primary prevention programs narrowly on suicide.

The goals also seem ideal for any school in general which is attempting to be a good educational environment, goals which most schools fall far short of. What is needed are specific proposals on what schools and their staff can do to promote the goals. For example, who would not wish to give each and every student opportunities to be successful and to feel valued and affirmed, but how should this be done in the day-to-day realities of teaching in a typical school?

Many students make use of the less-than-perfect opportunities that a typical school provides and develop into healthy adults. The retreatist students fail at or avoid these opportunities. If the school were to provide better programs, the retreatist students might still continue to fail at or avoid the programs. What is needed, perhaps, is staff specially hired to attend to these retreatist students.

In the delinquency prevention programs, the social workers had to work with the delinquents on their turf. However, using social workers from outside the community may have prejudiced the programs against success at the outset. It would seem that the staff in a primary prevention program should be acceptable to the retreatist students, perhaps students themselves, and they have to be able to work with the retreatists on their territory. Many suicide prevention programs use "like to counsel like." For example, a recent suicide prevention program in Trenton State Prison uses inmates to identify and counsel other inmates (Gammage, 1990).

But the present recommendations go beyond suicide prevention, suggesting that the broader issues of self-esteem, values clarification, bonding to social networks and other important development tasks be addressed. If these basic problems are tackled, many kinds of problems (including drug and alcohol abuse, suicide and delinquency) may be considerably reduced.

REFERENCES

Brager, G., & Purcell, F. (Eds.) *Community action against poverty.* New Haven, CT: College & University Press, 1967.

Cloward, R., & Ohlin, L. *Delinquency and opportunity.* New York: Free Press, 1960.

Cohen, A. *Delinquent boys.* New York: Free Press, 1955.

Durkheim, E. *Le suicide.* Paris: Felix Alcan, 1897.

Gammage, J. Prison peers fight against suicide. *The Philadelphia Inquirer,* 1990, May 6, 1B, 7B.

Gastil, R. Homicide and a regional culture of violence. *American Sociological Review,* 1971, 36, 412–427.

Kobrin, S. The Chicago Area Project. *Annals of the American Academy of Political & Social Science,* 1959, 322, 19–29.

Kreitman, N., Smith, P., & Eng-Seong, T. Attempted suicide as language. *British Journal of Psychiatry,* 1970, 116, 465–473.

Lester, D. Southern subculture, personal violence (suicide and homicide), and firearms. *Omega,* 1986–1987, 17, 183–186.

Lester, D. A subcultural theory of teenage suicide. *Adolescence,* 1987a, 22, 317–320.

Lester, D. An availability-acceptability theory of suicide. *Activitas Nervosa Superior,* 1987b, 29, 164–166.

Lester, D. A regional analysis of suicide and homicide rates in the USA. *Social Psychiatry & Psychiatric Epidemiology,* 1988, 23, 202–205.

Lester, D. Depression and suicide in college students and adolescents. *Personality & Individual Differences,* 1990, in press.

Livermore, A. Forty suicide notes. *Proceedings of the 18th Annual Meeting.* Denver: American Association of Suicidology, 1985, pp. 47–49.

Marks, A., & Abernathy, T. Toward a sociocultural perspective on means of self-destruction. *Life-Threatening Behavior,* 1974, 4, 3–17.

Marks, A., & Stokes, C. Socialization, firearms and suicide. *Social Problems,* 1976, 23, 622–629.

Merton, R. *Social theory and social structure.* Glencoe, IL: Free Press, 1957.

Miller, W. Lower class culture as a generating milieu of gang delinquency. *Journal of Social Issues,* 1958, 14, 5–19.

Miller, W. The impact of a "total community" delinquency control project. *Social Problems,* 1962, 10, 168–191.

Morgan, H., Pocock, H., & Pottle, S. The urban distribution of non-fatal deliberate self-harm. *British Journal of Psychiatry,* 1975, 126, 319–328.

Patrick, S. K. School focussed suicide prevention. In D. Lester (Ed.), *Suicide '89.* Denver: American Association of Suicidology, 1989, pp. 132–135.

Philip, A. E., & McCulloch, J. W. Use of social indices in psychiatric epidemiology. *British Journal of Preventive & Social Medicine,* 1966, 20, 122–126.

Platt, S. A subculture of parasuicide? *Human Relations,* 1985, 38, 257–297.

Platt, S., Hawton, K., Kreitman, N., Fagg, J., & Foster, J. Recent clinical and epidemiological trends in parasuicide in Edinburgh and Oxford. *Psychological Medicine,* 1988, 18, 405–418.

Rainer, R. J. Summary of a two-year pilot prevention/intervention-suicide/depression program covering grades kindergarten through 12th. In D. Lester (Ed.), *Suicide '89.* Denver: American Association of Suicidology, 1989, pp. 117–119.

Sellin, T. *Culture, conflict, and crime.* New York: Social Science Research Council, 1938.

Shaw, C. R., & McKay, H. D. *Juvenile delinquency and urban areas.* Revised edition. Chicago: University of Chicago Press, 1972.

Stack, S. The effects of interstate migration on suicide. *International Journal of Social Psychiatry,* 1980a, 26, 17–25.

Stack, S. The effects of marital dissolution on suicide. *Journal of Marriage & the Family,* 1980b, 42, 83–91.

Stephens, B. J. The social relationships of women. In D. Lester (Ed.), *Why women kill themselves.* Springfield, IL: Charles C Thomas, 1988, pp. 73–85.

Wolfgang, M. E., & Ferracuti, F. *The subculture of violence.* London: Tavistock, 1967.

Chapter 5

A LEARNING THEORY OF SUICIDE

The theories discussed in the previous chapter proposed that the structure of the society was a primary cause of crime and delinquency. In contrast, the theories described in this and the following chapter focus on *social processes*, the relationships between the individual and people in the society, such as parents, teachers, friends, and so on. Thus, these theories have a socio-psychological orientation, stressing such factors as the learning of criminal attitudes, feelings of alienation from society, and a poor self-concept.

There are two major types of social process theory. *Learning theories* hold that crime is learned from one's associates and friends. *Social control theory* holds that delinquency and crime are the result of disrupted ties between the individual and the major institutions of the society—family, peers and school. In this chapter we will review the learning theories and discuss their implications for suicide.

Differential Association Theory

Sutherland (1947) proposed that criminal behavior was learned in interaction with other persons. People do not become criminals simply by living in a particular type of society. Criminal, and other deviant patterns of behavior, are actively learned by people from others who serve as teachers and guides. This learning occurs primarily within intimate personal groups. It is family members, friends, and peers who have the most influence.

The learning covers the techniques of committing the crime as well as the specific motives, drives, rationalizations and attitudes. (Thus, criminals come to hold different values and attitudes from those held by law-abiding people.) People have to be coached on how to pick a lock or shoplift, as well as learning how to react to their crimes and their victims. If more of the person's friends and family are violating the law rather than following the law, the balance is tipped in favor of the person

58

becoming a law violator. Furthermore, the quality and intensity of the person's relationships with the potential teachers and guides is critical. The more durable relationships have more influence on the person, as do those that occur at a young age, and the prestige of the potential teacher increases the likelihood of learning.

Sutherland thought that the mechanism of learning criminal behavior was no different from the mechanisms responsible for learning any behavior. As psychologists, we would expect classical conditioning, operant conditioning, imitation and modeling, and insight learning all to play a role.

Neutralization Theory

Sykes and Matza (1957; Matza, 1964) proposed a theory which has come to be known as *neutralization theory* or *drift theory*. They proposed that delinquents hold values and attitudes similar to those of law-abiding people, but they learn techniques which enable them to neutralize these values and attitudes temporarily when committing crimes. The potential criminal learns through his interactions with others to disregard the controlling influences of the society's social rules.

On a continuum from total freedom to total constraint, most people lie somewhere in the middle, but we can move toward one end or the other depending upon our state of mind or the social situation we are in. This movement is called drift. The delinquent subculture encourages drift toward the freedom end of the continuum, and it provides a set of justifications for the violations of law and order.

The techniques of neutralization include:

(1) denial of responsibility—the act was not their fault or was due to forces beyond their control. "It wasn't my fault."

(2) denial of criminal intent—they were not stealing, they were borrowing—or they did not mean to damage the property, they were simply playing. "I didn't mean to do it."

(3) denigration of the victim—the crime may be justified by disparaging the victim—he was an offensive authority figure or a member of an outgroup (such as a homosexual)—the owner of the property was absent. "He had it coming to him."

(4) condemning the moral authorities—police are seen as brutal oppres-

sors and judges as corrupt—teachers and parents are unfair. "Why pick on me? Politicians get away with it."

(5) appealing to higher loyalites—seeing loyalty to their peer group as more important than following the rules of the larger society. "I had to help my buddy."

A Learning Theory of Suicide

Although a learning theory of suicide had been tentatively suggested before (Frederick and Resnick, 1971; Diekstra, 1974), Lester (1987) presented the strongest case possible for a learning theory of suicide.

A simple learning theory of human behavior uses the same learning paradigms that have been identified by psychologists who experimented with lower animals in laboratory research. It is assumed that these paradigms are appropriately applicable to humans, and that humans learn behaviors in the same way as these lower animals learn.

Two major learning paradigms have been identified over the years. First, in *classical conditioning,* previously neutral stimuli (the conditioned stimuli) become associated with other stimuli (the unconditioned stimuli) that produce responses. Eventually, after many pairings, the formerly neutral stimuli now elicit the response.

The second major learning paradigm is *operant conditioning.* In operant conditioning, if a response is made in the presence of a stimulus and is followed by a reinforcer (or reward), then the response is more likely to be emitted in the presence of the stimulus in the future. Reinforcers are of two kinds. Positive reinforcers are the onset of something nice, whereas negative reinforcers are the ending of something nasty.

Social learning theory (Bandura, 1977) modified simple learning theory by taking into account the fact that humans have thoughts, beliefs and expectations which can affect the simple learning paradigms described above. Thoughts can provide stimuli, responses can be imagined and reinforcers can be cognitions (such as self-praise).

Learning to be Depressed

There are three major learning theories of depression. Lewinsohn (1974) has argued that depression is caused by a lack of reinforcement. For example, responses that were rewarded in the past are no longer rewarded, because the source of the rewards may no longer be present. A spouse may have died, children may have moved away, or a job may have been lost through being laid off or through retirement. Without these positive reinforcers, the person no longer performs the responses that were formerly rewarded. The person, therefore, becomes passive and withdrawn. Ferster (1974), too, has conceptualized depressed people as those who fail to stay in effective contact with the rewards of their environment and who fail to avoid its aversive aspects. In particular, depressed people are failing to obtain adequate amounts of reinforcement.

Seligman (1974) argued that depression was a manifestation of a phenomenon that he called learned helplessness. Seligman exposed dogs to inescapable electric shock. When he then permitted these dogs to escape the painful electric shocks, they did not learn to do so. In contrast, dogs not previously exposed to the inescapable electric shock soon learned to escape the electric shocks. Seligman suggested that the dogs who were forced to endure inescapable electric shock had learned to be helpless, that is, they had learned that the shock was always inescapable. The experience of previous failure caused them to make little effort in the future. In human depression, therefore, it has been argued that in psychologically painful situations, the person tried to escape the pain but failed. He then generalized from this experience and learned (or decided) that he could never escape the pain.

Frederick and Resnick (1971) noted that depression may be rewarded by significant others. Depressed behaviors may elicit positive reinforcers from others such as caretaking behaviors, the so-called secondary gain. Furthermore, parents may actually punish the child for aggressive responses, thereby facilitating the inhibition of the outward expression of anger. This blocked anger may then be turned inward onto the self and manifest itself as depression, the traditional psychoanalytic view of depression.

Learning Suicidal Behavior

Operant conditioning paradigms may explain attempts at and threats of suicide. Suicidal behavior has often been viewed as a manipulative behavior. Indeed, Farberow and Shneidman's (1961) classic book on attempted suicide was called *The Cry For Help*, drawing attention to the desire to manipulate the environment by means of the suicidal act. Sifneos (1966), too, studied attempted suicides and was struck by the manipulative aspects of their behavior. 66 percent were judged to have used manipulation (that is, tried to prevent another from leaving thereby interrupting the relationship, or tried to control another person's actions in some way).

Operant conditioning may similarly explain attempts at and threats of suicidal behavior. There are many possible positive reinforcers for suicidal behavior, including increased attention from significant others, expressions of concern (and even love), and the possibility of making others suffer. Negative reinforcers can include being removed from a stressful situation into a hospital (medical or psychiatric) and relief of tension. The reinforcement in the situations is obtained quite quickly, making it more potent.

The use of a suicide as a manipulative act, in order to extort particular responses from others, may lead to a sequence in which the severity of successive suicide actions has to increase in order to keep extorting the desired response from others. Lester et al. (1978) found that attempted suicides who later completed suicide did indeed increase their suicidal intent (as measured by an objective scale based upon the circumstances of the suicidal act) in their final suicidal action from that of the earlier attempt. More detailed studies of the suicidal intent of repeated suicide attempters need to be carried out.

Such manipulative behavior may have been learned in childhood and adolescence. A child may learn to hurt himself in order that he can manipulate others by getting a positive response from his parents to his self-injuries. For example, a parent who "suffers" because of misdeeds of his child, such as the child failing academic work, teaches the child that he can make others suffer (anxiety, grief, or rage) by doing things that admittedly are also self-injurious.

Suicide as a Failure in Socialization

In most cultures suicide is frowned upon. Indeed, in some it is a sin. Furthermore, in any culture, suicide is rare. For example, Hungary has one of the highest suicide rates in the world. Yet its rate is only about 40 per 100,000 people per year. Suicide is always a statistically deviant act. This suggests that suicidal individuals may be non-socialized. Those who kill themselves have not been socialized into the traditional non-suicidal culture. Thus, on psychological tests of socialization and conformity, suicidal individuals should appear to be relatively unsocialized. Of course, Durkheim's (1897) ideas on suicide included the notion that suicide would be especially common in those who were relatively poorly socially integrated and poorly socially regulated. He called these types of suicide egotistic and anomic, respectively.

This factor (of being poorly socialized into the traditional non-suicidal culture) may be a necessary, but not sufficient factor. For the non-socialized person, peers and role models provide a crucial input. Those who are non-socialized will often be associated with other similarly non-socialized people. Thus, this non-socialized group forms its own small subculture. This subculture may share the information necessary for suicide. What methods to use? How many pills to take?

Role models, whether familiar friends or mythic heroes, provide models for non-conformity. When a Marilyn Monroe and a Freddie Prinze completes suicide, they act as role models for the ordinary person. And when one teenager in a school completes suicide, it occasionally leads to further suicides among the peer group.

There is evidence too that the chronic suicide attempter is a social deviant who comes from locales where social deviance is common (Lester, 1983). Families in these areas often fail to discipline their children and fail to teach them the values of the larger society. They also fail to encourage them in interests and activities which would serve as deterrents to deviant behavior.

Such a child typically grows up without acquiring the attitudes and skills for achieving long-term goals. The person then turns to short-term methods for achieving goals, such as drugs, delinquent behavior, and suicide attempts. There may also be a sex difference here, with males choosing behaviors such as drugs and crime more often, while females choose suicide attempts. (Females in these locales also have a high rate of illegitimate births.) A suicide attempt for such a person is a cathartic act and one which often brings about an immediate response from others.

An interesting question is why people in these locales turn to suicide rather than drugs or criminal behavior, given the predisposing factors. It may be that the choice is sex-linked as mentioned above. It may also be related to such factors as the availability of drugs in the area, the presence of a support group (or gang), and parental models.

Childhood Experiences of Punishment

There is some evidence that a child's experience of punishment may be critical in determining whether he learns to express his aggression outwards or whether he learns to inhibit this outward expression of aggression, turning it inward upon himself (Henry and Short, 1954).

Henry and Short showed how experience of love-oriented punishment dealt out by the parent who is the source of nurturance and love leads to the development of tendencies to inhibit the primary other-oriented expression of aggression. When the source of nurturance and love also administers the punishment, then the primary other-oriented expression of aggression threatens to end the flow of love and nurturance. If the child retaliates, he will receive no nurturance. Therefore, the child develops habits of inhibiting this primary other-oriented aggression.

Similarly, punishing a child by threatening to withdraw love also causes the child to inhibit his anger at being punished, since expression of that anger may lead also to loss of love. Such children may be prone later in life to depression and suicide.

Suicide as a Result of the Ineffectiveness of Adaptive Coping Skills

Jacobs (1971) has presented a thorough study of the progressive disintegration of the life of the suicidal adolescent. He looked at the number and type of debilitating events experienced by suicidal and non-suicidal adolescents and found that although the suicidal adolescents had experienced a greater total number of such events (for example, residential moves, breakup of romances, hospitalizations, and so on), the difference in the frequency of such events was most marked after the onset of adolescence. Thus, not only were the suicidal adolescents subjected to a more extensive and intensive history of problems but also the problems did not diminish in adolescence.

To investigate how the adolescents attempted to cope with the events that they experienced, Jacobs looked at the onset of behavioral problems during adolescence. The suicidal adolescents had experienced significantly more behavioral problems than the control adolescents. Both groups resorted to behavior problems classified as "rebellion" to the same degree. The suicidal adolescents, however, tended to show "withdrawal into self" and "physical withdrawal" significantly more than the control adolescents. Jacobs interpreted this withdrawal to indicate the alienation of the suicidal adolescent from his parents. Jacobs also found that the suicidal adolescents had a greater onset of behavioral problems during adolescence (that is, during the escalation phase).

Jacobs found that the adolescents generally used adaptive techniques in trying to deal with the problems at home before turning to maladaptive techniques such as running away and attempting suicide. Only one adolescent attempted suicide without ever resorting to other techniques (and his problems were different, in that they stemmed primarily from ill health). Thus, these suicidal adolescents turned to suicide because their significant others failed to respond to the more adaptive coping skills.

Differential Association: Suicide in Significant Others

A social learning theory of suicide would be immeasurably strengthened if it could be shown that suicidal behavior was frequent in the families, relatives and friends of suicidal individuals. This would provide the basis for an imitation effect. It would give the suicidal person a chance to learn about suicide as a strategy by watching others engage in the behavior and by observing the effects of the behavior. What evidence is there for this?

Six reports have appeared which report an excess of suicides in the families, relatives and friends of suicidal people (Corder et al., 1974; Diekstra, 1974; Garfinkel et al., 1979; Hauschild, 1968; Murphy et al., 1969; Woodruff et al., 1972). On the other hand, eight studies have found no differences (Doroff, 1969; Finlay, 1970; Hill, 1969; Johnson and Hunt, 1979; Pokorny, 1960; Rorsman, 1973; Rosen, 1970; Tucker and Reinhardt, 1966).

In addition, Pollack (1938) compared attempted suicides with completed suicides and found a greater incidence of completed suicide in the families of the completed suicides. Ettlinger (1964) compared attempted suicides who subsequently killed themselves with those who did not and found no significant differences in the incidence of completed suicide in the family members.

Winokur et al. (1973) compared depressed inpatients with an early onset of the disorder to those who had a late onset of the disorder. The early onset patients had more parents who had completed suicide than the late-onset patients had. This was especially so for the female patients.

It is sometimes difficult to make sense of research that is inconsistent. Six studies found an excess of suicidal behavior in the significant others of suicidal people, while eight studies found no differences. Perhaps it is noteworthy that no study found a lower incidence of suicide in the significant others of suicidal individuals? The fourteen studies, therefore, seem to indicate an excess (albeit a modest excess) of suicidal behavior in the significant others of suicidal people.

One final study seems especially pertinent to the present discussion. Sletten et al. (1973) found an excess of attempted suicides (but not completed suicides) in the relatives of attempted suicides and an excess of completed suicides (but not attempted suicides) in the relatives of completed suicides. No one appears to have tried to replicate the specificity of this result, but, if it proves replicable, it would provide powerful evidence for a social learning theory of suicide.

Kreitman et al. (1969) predicted that those who had attempted suicide would have more kin and close friends who were suicidal than would non-suicidal individuals. They traced a sample of contacts of attempted suicides and found a greater incidence of suicide attempts than would be expected on the basis of chance in these contacts. The phenomenon was especially strong in those less than 35 years of age and in those attempting suicide with drugs. These data could indicate either the effects of suggestion and imitation and support the social learning theory of suicide or could merely reflect the mutual attraction between suicidal individuals so that they associate together.

There appears to be good evidence that suicidal behavior is common in the relatives and friends of suicidal people. However, it is far from clear why the results of the different studies are inconsistent. Furthermore, the importance of the type of suicidal behavior is not well established. That is, do attempted and completed suicides have different patterns of suicidal behavior in their significant others? Sletten's result that completed suicide had an excess of completed suicide in significant others while attempted suicides had an excess of attempted suicides is intriguing but in need of replication.

The Role of Suggestion in Suicide

Barraclough et al. (1977) found an increase in the number of suicides in Portsmouth, England, after a newspaper story about a suicide, but this increase was found only for males below the age of forty-four.

Phillips (1974) found that front-page newspaper stories on suicide increased the number of suicides in the following month. The rise was found only in the region served by the newspaper. Philips found no increase in the number of suicides in the month following a presidential death. There was no subsequent dip in the number of suicides each month, and so Phillips concluded that newspaper publicity creates additional suicides rather than speeding up suicide in those who would have killed themselves anyway.

There have been several critiques of Philips's research, but no alternative analyses of his data have been presented. Thus, it seems very likely that newspaper publicity of suicide stories does cause a rise in the suicide rate in the following week.

Stack (1987) has pursued this research and found that suicides increase in the week following the suicide of an entertainment celebrity and, to a lesser extent, the suicide of an an American political figure. However, the suicides of artists and foreign people have little or no impact.

Phillips (1982) studied the effects of suicides in soap operas on suicide in the general population. He found more suicides (and motor vehicle fatalities) in the week in which a soap opera suicide occurred as compared to the previous week. Bollen and Phillips (1982) next looked at the effect of television news coverage of actual suicides. Again, they found an increase in the number of suicides in the following week as compared to the previous week.

Epidemics of Suicide

Imitation does appear to play a role in "epidemics" of suicidal behavior. Hankoff (1961) reported an epidemic of attempted suicide in a Marine base overseas. The attempts were clustered in time, and the methods used were similar in each cluster. Examination of one cluster in detail showed that the first attempt had resulted in maximum secondary gain (hospitalization and removal from duty), whereas the last attempt resulted in the least secondary gain. Hankoff implied that, as rewards from attempting suicide declined, the Marines dropped that behavior as a means of procuring relief. Crawford and Willis (1966) found evidence of imitation in three pairs of suicides that took place in a hospital but no evidence in three other pairs of suicides. Niemi (1975) found that completed suicides in Finnish prisons occurred within two days of each other more often than would be expected by chance. Coleman (1987) has reported many cases of suicide clusters that appear to show imitation, including many recent clusters of teenagers, but some investigators doubt that all clusters reflect imitation (Selkin, 1986).

Conclusions

Lester (1987) concluded that the evidence reviewed above is strongly supportive of the possibility that suicide is, at least in part, a learned behavior. In his book, where there was more space to explore the issue, Lester reviewed additional lines of research which support this position, such as cultural differences in suicide and the factors which appear to determine the choice of method for suicide.

Neutralization Effects in Suicide

There is much less evidence currently available for a neutralization theory of suicide. For example, do suicides show denial of the sort that would facilitate them committing a suicidal act? Only two studies appear to be relevant to this.

First, Spiegel and Neuringer (1963) compared genuine suicide notes with notes written by non-suicidal individuals pretending that they were about to kill themselves (simulated notes). They found that the genuine notes mentioned the word "suicide" or suicide synonyms less often than the simulated notes, and they interpreted this to mean that the suicidal people were trying to deceive themselves about their imminent suicide and to concentrate on things other than suicide.

Jacobs (1982) focussed upon the moral justification for suicide. Jacobs introduced the notion of trust violation, the individual's violation of the sacred trust of life. As a result of this trust violation, the individual who is going to kill himself must reconcile the image of himself as a to-be-trusted person with the fact that he is about to break that trust through his act of suicide. Jacobs examined suicide notes to document this process.

Jacobs proposed the following sequence for the suicidal process: the person (a) is faced with extremely distressing problems, (b) views this state of affairs as part of a long history of such distressing crises, (c) believes that death is the only solution to these problems, (d) has become increasingly socially isolated so that he cannot share his distress with others, (e) has overcome his internalized moral constraints that categorize suicide as irrational or immoral, (f) has succeeded in this since his social isolation makes him feel less constrained by societal rules, (g) constructs some verbal rationalization than enables him to view himself as a to-be-trusted person in spite of his trust violation by defining the problem as not of his own making or as open to no other solution, and (h) makes some provision that his problems will not occur after death.

The authors of the most common form of notes characteristically beg forgiveness or request indulgence, show that the problem is not of their making, note the history of the problem, communicate that the problems have grown beyond endurance, note the necessity of death, and communicate that they are fully aware of what they are doing but know that the reader will not understand their reasons.

In order to take precautions that the life after death will be free from problems, Jacobs noted that there are several courses open to the suicidal person. He sometimes stops attending church and becomes an atheist, thereby disposing of heaven and hell. Occasionally, he tries to find consensual evidence from others that God forgives everything (including suicide) and so becomes very religious, or he can merely suppress the knowledge that God will not forgive. Another alternative is to persuade oneself that even hell will be better than the present life on earth. Often, the suicidal person will ask God for forgiveness in the suicide note and request others to pray for his soul. Finally, the individual may come to believe in reincarnation, thereby forcing out of awareness conventional religious beliefs.

Apart from these two studies, no other research has focussed on what an individual must do to overcome what are obviously for the vast majority of people the inhibitions against suicide. This is an area that would appear to warrant investigation in the future.

Implications for Suicide Prevention

A learning theory of suicide has several implications for preventing suicide. One of the major thrusts of the differential association theory of delinquency is that a person learns the values and attitudes that go with criminal behavior from family, friends and peers. Extending this to suicide means that the learning about suicide as a strategy for solving problems from one's social network must be discouraged.

When a suicide occurs, there are close family, relatives, friends and colleagues who must cope with the thoughts and feelings aroused by this act. Often it is found, for example, that suicide runs in families. Although the possibility of a genetic predisposition toward psychiatric disorder may often be present in such families, the impact of learning cannot be discounted.

For example, Ernest Hemingway's grandfather tried to shoot himself. Ernest's father did commit suicide with a gun, and three of the six children also committed suicide. Ernest and his brother Leicester both shot themselves, while Sunny took a lethal overdose (Lester, 1987). Before this sequence is dismissed as simply the result of an inherited affective disorder, it should be noted that all of the suicides occurred in old age when the people were suffering from severe physical illnesses. Thus, it seems likely that the Hemingways learned that suicide is an appropriate strategy for dealing with this situation.

Interestingly, while there are many cases in which, for example, the

.ild of suicide later killed himself (such as Ernest Hemingway or the .merican poet John Berryman), there are also cases where the children of the suicide did not (such as the basketball player Larry Bird and the television executive Ted Turner). It would be of great interest to determine the psychological differences between these two groups of individuals so that we can better understand why only some children of suicides subsequently choose suicide.

Thus, intervention with the survivors of suicide would seem necessary to prevent this learning from taking place. Such intervention, besides accomplishing typical psychotherapeutic movement, should focus specifically on teaching alternative strategies for coping with crises and on weakening the neutralization processes that may precede the choice of suicide.

The same intervention techniques seem to be called for in any small community in which one or more suicides have taken place, such as a school, church group, hospital ward, psychotherapeutic group, small community, or native American reservation.

It might be useful for interveners in these situations to have a clearer idea of what neutralization techniques suicidal people use (and this could be clarified by further research on the topic) and in what ways these neutralization techniques can be inhibited.

REFERENCES

Bandura, A. *Social learning theory.* Englewood Cliffs, NJ: Prentice-Hall, 1977.

Barraclough, B. M., Shepherd, D., & Jennings, C. Do newspaper reports of coroners' inquests incite people to commit suicide? *British Journal of Psychiatry,* 1977, 131, 528–532.

Bollen, K., & Phillips, D. Imitative suicides. *American Sociological Review,* 1982, 47, 802–809.

Coleman, L. *Suicide clusters.* Boston: Faber & Faber, 1987.

Corder, B., Page, P., & Corder, R. Parental history, family communication and interaction patterns in adolescent suicide. *Family Therapy,* 1974, 1, 285–290.

Crawford, J., & Willis, J. Double suicide in psychiatric hospital patients. *British Journal of Psychiatry,* 1966, 112, 1231–1235.

Diekstra, R. A social learning theory approach to the prediction of suicidal behavior. *Proceedings of the 7th International Congress for Suicide Prevention.* Amsterdam: Swets & Zeitlinger BV, 1974.

Doroff, D. Attempted and gestured suicide in adolescent girls. *Dissertation Abstracts,* 1969, 27B, 2631.

Durkheim, E. *Le suicide.* Paris: Felix Alcan, 1897.

Ettlinger, R. Suicide in a group of patients who had previously attempted suicide. *Acta Psychiatrica Scandinavia*, 1964, 40, 364–378.

Farberow, N. L., & Shneidman, E. S. *The cry for help*. New York: McGraw-Hill, 1961.

Ferster, C. Behavioral approaches to depression. In R. J. Friedman & M. M. Katz (Eds.), *The psychology of depression*. Washington, DC: Winston, 1974.

Finlay, S. Suicide and self-injury in Leeds University students. *Proceedings of the 5th International Conference for Suicide Prevention*. Vienna: IASP, 1970.

Frederick, C., & Resnick, H. How suicidal behaviors are learned. *American Journal of Psychotherapy*, 1971, 25, 37–55.

Garfinkel, B., Froese, A., & Golombek, H. Suicidal behavior in a pediatric population. *Proceedings of the 10th International Congress for Suicide Prevention*. Ottawa: IASP, 1979.

Hankoff, L. An epidemic of attempted suicide. *Comprehensive Psychiatry*, 1961, 2, 294–298.

Hauschild, T. Suicidal population of a military psychiatric center. *Military Medicine*, 1968, 133, 425–437.

Henry, A. F., & Short, J. F. *Suicide and homicide*. Glencoe, IL: Free Press, 1954.

Hill, O. The association of childhood bereavement with suicide in depressive illnesses. *British Journal of Psychiatry*, 1969, 115, 159–164.

Jacobs, J. *Adolescent suicide*. New York: Wiley, 1971.

Jacobs, J. *The moral justification of suicide*. Springfield, IL: Charles C Thomas, 1982.

Johnson, G., & Hunt, G. Suicidal behavior in bipolar manic-depressive patients and their families. *Comprehensive Psychiatry*, 1979, 20, 159–164.

Kreitman, N., Smith, P., & Tan, E. Attempted suicide in social networks. *British Journal of Preventive & Social Medicine*, 1969, 23, 116–123.

Lester, D. *Why people kill themselves*. Springfield, IL: Charles C Thomas, 1983.

Lester, D. *Suicide as a learned behavior*. Springfield, IL: Charles C Thomas, 1987.

Lester, D., Beck, A. T., & Narrett, S. Suicidal intent in successive suicidal actions. *Psychological Reports*, 1978, 43, 110.

Lewinsohn, P. A behavioral approach to depression. In R. J. Friedman & M. M. Katz (Eds.), *The psychology of depression*. New York: Halstead, 1977.

Matza, D. *Delinquency and drift*. New York: Wiley, 1964.

Murphy, G. E., Wetzel, R., Swallow, C., & McClure, J. Who calls the suicide prevention center? *American Journal of Psychiatry*, 1969, 126, 314–324.

Niemi, T. The time-space distance of suicides committed in the lock-up in Finland in 1963–1967. *Psychiatria Fennica*, 1975, 267–270.

Phillips, D. The influences of suggestion on suicide. *American Sociological Review*, 1974, 39, 340–354.

Phillips, D. The impact of fictional television stories on U.S. adult fatalities. *American Journal of Sociology*, 1982, 87, 1340–1359.

Pokorny, A. D. Characteristics of 44 patients who subsequently committed suicide. *Archives of General Psychiatry*, 1960, 2, 314–323.

Pollack, B. A study of the problem of suicide. *Psychiatric Quarterly*, 1938, 12, 306–330.

Rorsman, B. Suicide in psychiatric patients. *Social Psychiatry*, 1973, 8, 55–66.

Rosen, D. The serious suicide attempt. *American Journal of Psychiatry,* 1970, 127, 764–770.

Seligman, M. Depression and learned helplessness. In R. J. Friedman & M. M. Katz (Eds.), *The psychology of depression.* New York: Halstead, 1974.

Selkin, J. Probe of suicides points way to prevention. *Network News,* 1986, #4, 14.

Sifneos, P. Manipulative suicide. *Psychiatric Quarterly,* 1966, 40, 525–537.

Sletten, I., Evenson, R., & Brown, M. Some results from an automated statewide comparison among attempted, committed and nonsuicidal patients. *Life-Threatening Behavior,* 1973, 3, 191–197.

Spiegel, D., & Neuringer, C. Role of dread in suicidal behavior. *Journal of Abnormal & Social Psychology,* 1963, 66, 507–511.

Stack, S. Celebrities and suicide. *American Sociological Review,* 1987, 52, 401–412.

Sutherland, E. H. *Principles of criminology.* Philadelphia: Lippincott, 1947.

Sykes, G., & Matza, D. Techniques of neutralization. *American Sociological Review,* 1957, 22, 664–670.

Tucker, G., & Reinhardt, R. *Suicide attempts.* Pensacola, FL: US Naval Aerospace Medical Institute, 1966.

Winokur, G., Morrison, J., Clancy, J., & Crow, R. The Iowa 500. *Comprehensive Psychiatry,* 1973, 14, 99–106.

Woodruff, R., Clayton, P., & Guze, S. Suicide attempts and psychiatric diagnosis. *Diseases of the Nervous System,* 1972, 33, 616–621.

Chapter 6

A SOCIAL CONTROL THEORY OF SUICIDE

The second major type of social process theory of criminal behavior focusses on the ties between the individual on the one hand and conventional groups in the society, other law-abiding individuals, and the organizations and institutions of the society on the other. Those who have close relationships with parents, friends, and teachers are more likely to have a positive self-image and to be able to resist the temptation of crime. Those who feel detached from conventional society are unaffected by its social control functions. These theories are usually called *social control theories.*

The social controls may be internal or external. Internal controls involve such personality traits as a positive self-image and a strong internalized conscience. External controls involve positive close relationships with parents and with teachers who are conventional and law-abiding.

Social Bond Theory

Travis Hirschi (1969) assumed that all of us are potential criminals and that only social controls, not moral values, prevent us from behaving in a criminal manner. Hirschi noted four elements in the social bond between the individual and society.

(1) *Attachment* refers to the individual's interest in, sensitivity to, and caring for others, as well as concern for the wishes and expectations of others. The norms and values of the society are shared by the members, and if one cares about the reactions of others, then there is good reason to follow the norms.

Attachment to parents is the most important tie. If parents divorce or if one or both parents behave in such a way (abusively, for example) that the child's tie to them is weakened, then attachment will not take place. Without attachment to these first important people in our life (our parents), it is unlikely that the person will develop feelings of respect for others.

(2) *Commitment* refers to the time, energy and effort in pursuing conventional pursuits in our society. If the individual has a stake in society, then behaving deviantly endangers this. For example, if the person pursues an education, obtains a good job, seeks prestige and status, and becomes a property owner, then he will be less likely to engage in criminal behavior, because that would jeopardize his position in society.

(3) A person who is *involved* in conventional activities in society not only has less desire to engage in criminal behavior but he also has less time.

(4) Finally, the social bond involves *belief* in the moral validity of the norms established by society for himself. Those norms must be seen as both good and correct for society and as relevant to our own actions.

Hirschi found that high school students who felt close to their parents were less likely to engage in delinquent acts. Similarly, those who enjoyed and were successful in school were less likely to commit delinquent acts. Attachment to peers was also related, though less strongly, to avoidance of delinquent behavior.

Students with high educational and occupational aspirations were less likely to commit delinquent acts, as were those who spent more time in conventional activities such as homework. Finally, those students who had committed delinquent acts were just as likely to accept middle-class values as the students who avoided delinquent acts. Thus, the delinquent students held conventional values but apparently did not see the relevance of these values for themselves.

Two important findings from Hirschi's research were that the delinquent groups rarely recruited "good" boys and influenced them to turn bad and, secondly, that the delinquents did not have particularly warm or intimate relationships with one another.

Containment Theory

Walter Reckless (1967) focussed on internal controls as well as external controls. He noted that there were both pressures toward delinquency and away from it.

(1) *Inner containments* consisted of those forces in the personality resisting criminal involvement. People with a positive self-image, a strong ego, high frustration tolerance, goal orientation, and the ability to reduce

tension in socially acceptable ways are less likely to engage in criminal behavior.

(2) *Outer containments* are those normative rules and values that society possesses which restrain antisocial and criminal behavior. People with a sense of belonging, who are effectively supervised and disciplined, and who have a meaningful social role are less likely to commit criminal acts.

(3) *Internal pushes* are those forces within the individual which propel him toward criminal behavior, such as restlessness, hostility, rebellion, internal conflicts, and the need for immediate gratification.

(4) *External pulls* are those forces in society which pull the individual toward criminal acts such as deviant companions and the mass media.

(5) *External pressures* are those adverse social conditions which increase the likelihood of deviant behavior, such as poverty, unemployment, minority status, and limited opportunities.

Reckless proposed that the internal containments were more important than the external containments since we spend most of our time away from our family and the other groups supportive of social order. We have to rely most of the time, then, on our internal strengths to control our criminal impulses.

Social Control Theory and Crime Prevention

Control theory focusses on the role of the social bond in inhibiting delinquent behavior. Treatment of delinquents, then, should focus on strengthening this social bond. Family therapy would seem, therefore, to be crucial in preventing delinquent behavior. However, the adolescent's social bonding to his parents can hardly be strengthened without the cooperation of the parents.

Parents must be taught new ways of interacting with their children, punishment must be consistent and fair, and there must be an atmosphere of affection. In the absence of such parenting, ties with a surrogate such as a foster parent, big brother, more distant relative or even a detached gang worker must be built up.

Since detachment from the school is often associated with academic failure, the provision of remedial programs, specially trained instructors and parental involvement can help terminate the experience of failure. The impression we gain from the media portrayal of the successful educational programs is that often this success depends upon the skills of a charismatic teacher who bonds the adolescents to himself while engaged on some enterprise, whether it be athletics or a more intellectual pursuit such as chess or mathematics.

The criminal justice system should also behave, and appear to behave, fairly. If a youth feels that he is being treated unfairly or differently from others, then he will be more likely to detach himself from the values of society.

Some of the primary prevention programs related to these theories have tried to improve the school experience. The Alternative Learning Project in Rhode Island worked with educationally disillusioned students (Wall et al., 1981). There was a low student-teacher ratio, individualized programs, an emphasis on basic skills, special projects, and tutoring.

Government programs such as Head Start for preschoolers, Upward Bound for high school students, the Job Corps and CETA (Comprehensive Employment Training Act) programs can also be seen as consistent with the social control orientation.

A Social Control Theory of Suicide

The Social Level

The first major theory of suicide was proposed by Emile Durkheim (1897), who argued that suicide was caused by two social forces. *Social integration* referred to the degree to which individuals in the society were bound by social ties and relationships, while *social regulation* referred to the degree to which individuals had their desires and emotions controlled by the social values of the society. Durkheim held that suicide would be more likely if social integration was too weak (leading to egoistic suicide), if social regulation was too weak (leading to anomic suicide), or if these two social forces were too strong (leading to altruistic and fatalistic suicide, respectively).

Johnson (1965) noted that Durkheim both defined four types of suicide and made predictions about which social conditions led to high rates of suicide. Although altruistic and fatalistic make good sense as types of suicide, they are relatively rare. So Johnson proposed modifying Durkheim's theory, predicting that suicide would be more common if social integration and social regulation were weak.

It can be seen readily that Durkheim's theory focusses upon the social bond between the individual and society and so fits into social control theory. As a sociologist, Durkheim was not interested in the factors affecting the development of social integration and social regulation. However, he did point to a number of social processes that affected the strength of these two social forces, such as marriage versus divorce and religious affiliation.

Henry and Short (1954) developed a theory of suicide which focussed primarily upon the concept of social regulation, exploring which social and psychological factors legitimized other-oriented aggression (murder) versus self-oriented aggression (suicide). What enables the child to develop so that his primary response to frustration, that of other-oriented aggression, is seen as legitimate, while other children develop in such a way that this primary response is inhibited and self-directed aggression becomes legitimate?

Socially, the strength of external restraints was seen as the primary basis for legitimizing other-oriented aggression. When behavior is required to conform rigidly to the demands and expectations of others, the share of others in the responsibility for the consequences of the behavior increases, thereby legitimizing other-oriented aggression. When external restraints are weak, the self must bear the responsibility for the frustration generated, and other-oriented aggression fails to be legitimized.

Henry and Short proposed that, psychologically, low superego strength and low guilt were associated with the legitimization of other-oriented aggression. They suggested that this was fostered by the experience of physical punishment as a child as opposed to love-oriented punishment and also by having the same parent nurturing and punishing the child as opposed to one parent nurturing and the other parent punishing the child. Aggression against a parent who uses physical punishment merely increases the chance of another blow rather than threatening the supply of love, and aggression against the parent who administers punishment does not threaten the supply of love from the other parent who is the nurturer. In contrast, love-oriented punishment and punishment by the parent who nurtures the child would lead the child to inhibit their primary other-oriented aggressive response to frustration, since to aggress against the punisher in these situations would further threaten the supply of love and nurturance.

The Psychological Level

(1) THE SOCIAL BOND. It has long been known that suicide rates are highest among the divorced and the widowed and lowest for those who

married (Dublin, 1963). Completed suicide may also be less common ɪong people who have children (Breed, 1966). Ganzler (1967) found ɪat attempted suicides were experiencing greater social isolation than psychiatrically disturbed but non-suicidal patients. Furthermore, both Lester (1969) and Ganzler (1967) found that suicidal individuals rated their significant others more negatively than did non-suicidal individuals.

Lester's (1983) review of the literature found consistent evidence that suicidal individuals came from more disorganized homes and felt less close to their parents than non-suicidal individuals.

Perhaps the most comprehensive study of the degree to which child-parent bonds are disrupted in suicidal individuals was a study conducted by Jacobs (1971) on adolescent suicide attempters. He found that the adolescent suicide attempters had not merely experienced a broken home, for example, but that there was a long-standing history of problems in their families of which the broken home was but one incident. The parents of the suicidal adolescent were more likely to remarry and subsequently divorce than the parents of the non-suicidal teenagers. The parents of the suicidal adolescents were more likely to nag, yell and physically punish their children, and their children felt more alienated.

Thomas and Duszynski (1974) compared medical students who committed suicide later in their lives with those who did not and found that the suicides more often reported having emotionally undemonstrative parents and having felt less close to their parents.

(2) EGO STRENGTH. Several studies have reported low self-esteem in suicidal individuals. For example, Neuringer (1974) found that attempted suicides rated themselves as more negatively and others as more positively than did psychosomatic patients. Kaplan and Pokorny (1976) found that low self-esteem predicted subsequent suicidal ideation and suicidal attempts in seventh-grade children.

These reports of low self-esteem in suicidal individuals are consistent with reports of the high levels of depression and feelings of hopelessness in suicidal individuals (Beck et al., 1975).

Psychologists consider that perceiving yourself as responsible for both the good and the bad things that happen to you is a sign of psychological health. There is some evidence that suicidal people tend more often than non-suicidal people to have a belief in an external locus of control, that is, to believe that what happens to them is mainly due to chance or the influence of other people rather than as a result of what they themselves ester, 1983). A recent study reported, for example, that current suicidal ideation in college students was associated with beli‹ external locus of control, even after controlling for the level of sion (Lester, 1989).

Many authors have commented on impulsiveness in suicidal indiv.u uals. For example, Corder et al. (1974) found that adolescent suicide attempters were generally more impulsive and active than non-suicidal adolescents. Recently, Lester (1990) found that college students who had threatened suicide scored higher on a test of general impulsivity than equally depressed but non-suicidal college students. Epstein et al. (1973) found that medical students who subsequently committed suicide later in their lives were rated as more impulsive while in medical school.

Conclusions

It can be seen that a strong case can be made for a social control theory of suicide. Most of the sociological theorizing about suicide is really based on social controls, and a good deal of psychological research has pointed to the influence of poor relationships with parents, conflicts with lovers and friends, and social isolation on the development and appearance of suicidal behavior.

Suicidal people also appear to be deficient in internal controls. They have poor self-images and are seriously depressed, tend to be impulsive, and prone to blame others for their misfortunes.

Implications for Suicide Prevention

Community Action

The goals for suicide prevention in this perspective would be first to increase the social integration and social regulation of people. The society needs to discourage those actions which decrease social integration and regulation, such as divorce, and encourage those actions which increase social integration and regulation, such as church affiliation and social networking.

Those working in communities need to find ways to increase the social bonding for particular groups in society. Activities such as athletic leagues for kids and exercise and social groups for the elderly can provide primary prevention of alienation and anomie in a society. Interestingly some of the recent activities by city residents to drive drug dealers off their streets serve this function well. The residents on a street band together with a common goal and organize activities around this goal. These activities often include cleaning up the streets and actively being out on and socializing in the streets so that the drug dealers and purchasers find it easier to move elsewhere to conduct their transactions. Some cities have organized elections for street and block leaders to organize block parties and to beautify the city.

It is worth noting that often these types of activities are typically organized to combat a problem other than suicide and that they are often organized by religious and other activist groups. It does not seem likely that suicide prevention would ever serve as the stimulus for such activities, but suicide prevention may result incidentally from these action programs.

School Programs

Suicide prevention, along with the prevention of other disturbed and unproductive behaviors, can be facilitated by the development of schools which are attractive to children, an idea which has already been discussed in connection with the social structure perspective in Chapter 4. Schools must provide good role models in their teachers and must bond the children to the school by making school an interesting and pleasant place to be, goals which need not interfere with the educational functions.

Too many school teachers are incompetent. They are mediocre students graduating from state colleges who are unqualified for better positions. Too much of their time is taken up with discipline and keeping order in classes which are too large. Teachers needs to work more closely with smaller numbers of students, making learning exciting and interesting and demonstrating this by their own attitude to life.

Two examples of recent successful programs along these lines were given by Tifft (1990). One program set up classes for young black boys with no fathers at home. Attendance and academic performance improved and hostility decreased, but the program was halted because it violated civil rights laws. Another program has recruited black male professionals to come into the schools to work with children of both sexes. These are the types of programs which schools must offer, and not simply as special programs, but rather as part of the everyday routine of teaching and designed for all types of students.

The Family

Although it has long been accepted that we live in social groups and that psychotherapy with these larger groups might be more effective than working with individuals, family therapy has always been inhibited by the fact that many of those in a social group refuse to accept the need for therapy. The parents, brothers and sisters, and children of a disturbed individual often simply want the psychotherapist to take the disturbed individual and "cure" him or her. Getting them to be willing to participate, let alone be enthusiastic about participating, in family therapy is extremely difficult. Even when a family is motivated to come to family therapy, the motivation of some members decreases rapidly as the first signs of improvement appear.

However, the social control perspective requires that the bonds between the depressed and potentially suicidal individual and his or her family need to be developed and maintained in a psychological healthy style. Joseph Richman (1986) has recently written the first book dealing with the family treatment of suicidal individuals, and we must hope that this style of therapy becomes more and more common in the future.

Psychotherapy

Since some of the social controls against suicide must be internal, psychotherapy would seem useful in building a positive self-image, a strong ego, high frustration tolerance, and goal orientation. However, psychotherapy is going to affect only a small percentage of the population who might benefit from it.

Most individuals in a suicidal crisis who contact a mental health agency visit a suicide prevention and crisis service or a community mental health facility. These agencies typically use crisis intervention techniques often with a paraprofessional counselor. Crisis counseling is not designed for achieving the goals listed above.

In rare cases, agencies may operate groups for suicidal patients (Farberow, 1968). Because of the usefulness of increasing the social bonding of depressed and suicidal clients, group therapy may be preferable to individual psychotherapy for these clients, since social bonding is one of the major results of group psychotherapy (Yalom, 1970). However, group therapy run by professional therapists imposes limits on the clients, such as no social contact outside of the group and no romantic involvements between group members.

Given the ideas suggested by the social control perspective, it would seem useful to provide social network groups for depressed and suicidal people in addition to therapy groups, that is, groups whose function would be to help structure the time and activities of the clients outside of therapy hours. These social network groups could arrange evening meals, visits to movies, and other activities which would help bond the depressed and suicidal individuals to others in the social group.

The limitations of psychotherapy, either individual or group, are fine for clients who are not facing the decision of whether to commit suicide. However, for potentially suicidal clients more social support must be provided in addition to the psychotherapeutic experiences.

REFERENCES

Beck, A. T., Kovacs, M., & Weissman, A. Hopelessness and suicidal behavior. *Journal of the American Medical Association,* 1975, 234, 1146–1149.

Breed, W. Suicide, migration, and race. *Journal of Social Issues,* 1966, 22, 30–43.

Corder, B., Shorr, W., & Corder, R. A study of social and psychological characteristics of adolescent suicide attempters in an urban disadvantaged area. *Adolescence,* 1974, 9, 1–6.

Dublin, L. *Suicide.* New York: Ronald, 1963.

Durkheim, E. *Le suicide.* Paris: Felix Alcan, 1897.

Epstein, L., Thomas, C., Schaffer, J., & Perlin, S. Clinical predictors of physician suicide based on medical student data. *Journal of Nervous & Mental Disease,* 1973, 156, 19–29.

Farberow, N. L. Group psychotherapy with suicidal persons. In H. L. P. Resnick (Ed.), *Suicidal behaviors.* Boston: Little Brown, 1968.

Ganzler, S. Some interpersonal and social dimensions of suicidal behavior. *Dissertation Abstracts,* 1967, 28B, 1192–1193.

Henry, A. F., & Short, J. F. *Suicide and homicide.* New York: Free Press, 1954.

Hirschi, T. *Causes of delinquency.* Berkeley, CA: University of California, 1969.

Jacobs, J. *Adolescent suicide.* New York: Wiley, 1971.

Johnson, B. D. Durkheim's one cause of suicide. *American Sociological Review,* 1965, 30, 875–886.

Kaplan, H., & Pokorny, A. D. Self-derogation and suicide. *Social Science & Medicine,* 1976, 10, 113–121.

Lester, D. Resentment and dependency in the suicidal individual. *Journal of General Psychology,* 1969, 81, 137–145.

Lester, D. *Why people kill themselves.* Springfield, IL: Charles C Thomas, 1983.

Lester, D. Locus of control, depression and suicidal ideation. *Perceptual & Motor Skills,* 1989, 69, 1158.

Lester, D. Impulsivity in those who threaten suicide. *Personality & Individual Differences,* 1990, in press.

Neuringer, C. Self and other-appraisals by suicidal, psychosomatic and normal hospital patients. *Journal of Consulting & Clinical Psychology,* 1974, 42, 306.

Reckless, W. *The crime problem.* New York: Appleton-Century-Crofts, 1967.

Richman, J. *Family therapy for suicidal people.* New York: Springer, 1986.

Thomas, C., & Duszynski, K. Closeness to parents and the family constellation in a prospective study of five disease states. *Johns Hopkins Medical Journal,* 1974, 134, 251–270.

Tifft, S. Fighting the failure syndrome. *Time,* 1990, 135(21), 83–84.

Wall, J., Hawkins, J. D., Lishner, D., & Fraser, M. *Reports of the National Juvenile Justice Assessment Centers—juvenile delinquency prevention: a compendium of 36 program models.* Washington, DC: US Department of Justice, 1981.

Yalom, I. D. *The theory and practice of group psychotherapy.* New York: Basic Books, 1970.

Chapter 7

A SOCIAL REACTION THEORY OF SUICIDE

Social reaction theory is more commonly known as *labeling theory*. It focusses upon how other people in society react toward the delinquent. Most kids break the rules of society at one time or another, and many break the laws. A few of these kids get labeled. Some may be labeled by their parents, relatives, friends and teachers: "You're going to grow up and come to no good," "You are evil," and similar statements. Others will get formally processed by the criminal justice system and officially called juvenile delinquents. Social reaction theory focusses upon this informal and formal labeling process.

A person may be called many things as he grows up. For social reaction theory, there is sometimes a point at which the adolescent decides that a particular label is appropriate and accepts it. Once the label is accepted, then the person has truly entered on a "career."

The social reaction perspective draws our attention to the audience, to those who label others. It immediately makes it clear that labeling is culturally determined. What is unlawful in one society or in one group within a society may be acceptable in another. For example, bribery of public officials is punishable in some societies while considered the norm in others. Sexually promiscuous behavior is considered a delinquent behavior in American girls but not in American boys.

Social reaction theory, therefore, focusses on discrimination in the criminal justice system. Middle-class offenders are less likely to be labeled and less likely to be severely punished than lower-class offenders. Blacks and Hispanics may be treated differently than whites, and females treated differently than males.

Social reaction theory also inquires into the stigma of labels. The labels are usually quite long-lasting and involve a loss of status. The labeled person becomes a social outcast. This in turn leads to alienation from the mainstream of society and makes continuation of a criminal career even more likely. If you are an "X," then it is more pleasant to seek the company of others who are also labeled "Xs." Thus, labeling leads to the development of a new deviant identity and deviant subcultures. Individuals become what society says they are.

Edwin Lemert (1967) distinguished between primary and secondary deviance. Primary deviance is deviant behavior which is accepted by others. For example, a person may behave antisocially at a party when drunk. The behavior may be excused because the party constitutes a "time-out" from the rules of society and because the person was drunk. Primary deviance goes unlabeled by others and by the self.

However, some deviant behavior, especially if it is frequent or becomes organized into a role (or a career), becomes recognized as such and labeled by others and, eventually, the self. This is secondary deviance.

Becker (1963) classified people as either behaving deviantly or conventionally and being labeled as deviant or ignored, giving four types:

(1) The *conformist* behaves conventionally and is not labeled.
(2) The *falsely accused* behaves conventionally but gets labeled as deviant anyway.
(3) The *pure deviant* behaves in a deviant manner and gets so labeled.
(4) The *secret deviant* behaves in a deviant manner but does not get labeled, perhaps because people are not aware of the deviant behavior.

The social reaction theory has generated a great deal of research into the criminal justice system, especially on police discretion, prosecutorial decisions and sentencing, since these are the stages where labeling can take place. For example, when a police officer apprehends a suspect, he can let the youth go home with a warning or he can take him in and record the crime. This is the crucial first decision point in the criminal justice system.

The treatment implications of social reaction theory have centered around diversion (Schur, 1973). In diversion, efforts are made to keep youths out of the criminal justice system, especially if their crimes are minor. Such youths can be sent instead to community clinics, foster homes, job training or recreational programs, or educational programs. This would lessen the chances of them being labeled as delinquents and so deciding to enter a criminal career.

Labeling Theory and Psychiatric Disorder

Labeling theory has also assumed an important role in theories of psychiatric disturbance. Scheff (1966) argued that psychiatric disorder is in part a social role which is learned and that the reactions of others are the most important determinants of whether a person enters this role.

Again, many people behave deviantly in our society, and most of them do not get officially recognized. It is when this primary deviance comes to the attention of others who then label it that secondary deviance, that is, psychiatric disturbance, comes into existence.

Scheff considered the behaviors which people show that earn the label of "crazy." He noted that there were many rules in our society, most of which are written down somewhere and taught to children. There are criminal rules (recorded in state laws), moral rules (recorded in religious books), rules of etiquette (written down in books on social manners), and so on. It is illegal to steal, it is immoral to covet your neighbor's spouse, and you have to shake right hands on greeting people (not left hands).

In addition, Scheff argued that there were residual rules, rules left over which are not written down anywhere. It is when people break these residual rules that they run the risk of being labeled "crazy." For example, there is an unwritten rule in our society that you are not allowed to do nothing. You must always be doing something. Imagine you want to do nothing. How may you do this in public? Well you could sit with a book open in front of you. You appear to be reading. You may sit with a cigarette. You are smoking. You may get on a bus to a neighboring city and then get the bus back again. You appear to be traveling. You can put on a uniform, a swimsuit, and lay in the sun. You are sunbathing. You can wear some old clothes and lie in the gutter. You are a drunken bum. But you cannot do nothing!

If, in the middle of class, a student—or more impressively—a teacher simply stopped doing whatever he was doing and stared off into space, it would not be long before the school nurse or psychologist would be called to intervene.

It is when we break these residual rules that we run the risk of getting labeled as disturbed, and then there is the possibility that we will accept the label and decide to *be* psychiatrically disturbed.

As Scheff said, just as beauty is in the eye of the beholder, so is madness.

Others have made a similar point. R. D. Laing, for example, has documented cases of young women labeled as schizophrenic and who have become psychiatric inpatients, yet who are clearly not disturbed. Laing and Esterson (1964), for example, reported a case of a woman who accused the hospital staff of stealing her mail. Her mother vehemently claimed to her daughter that she wrote to her every day, but no letters arrived. The mother confessed privately to Laing that she had not written any letters. The daughter had a choice: to decide that her mother was a liar, or to believe her mother and claim that the hospital was withholding her mail. The latter choice may have seemed paranoid to the psychiatric staff, but it was a perfectly reasonable non-psychotic decision.

Braginsky et al. (1969) have argued that psychiatric patients learn about the life in psychiatric hospitals and decide to get admitted (though the choice may not necessarily be conscious). Once in the psychiatric hospital, they behave in such a way as to ensure that their desires are satisfied—to stay or leave, to work or play, and so on. They argue that schizophrenia, for example, is not a psychiatric *illness* but rather a term to describe people who have difficulty living in the world. Braginsky and his colleagues conducted several studies to demonstrate that chronic psychiatric patients fake severe psychiatric disturbance or minimal psychiatric disturbance depending on the outcomes they expect for having a certain severity of disturbance.

MacAndrew and Edgerton (1969) argued that the behavior of individuals when drunk was under conscious and rational control and that typically people misbehave when drunk only to the extent that they know will be excused by others the following morning (see also Critchlow, 1986). In a similar fashion, some scholars have suggested that alcoholism is under much more individual control than we would expect if alcoholism was a *medical illness* (Marlatt et al., 1973; Sobell et al., 1972).

The same issues that arise in the social reaction theory of delinquency arise here for psychiatric disorder. For example, it appears that Scott Fitzgerald was no less disturbed than his wife Zelda Fitzgerald. But Scott became the famous novelist, while Zelda became a psychiatric patient (Milford, 1970). The sexism of the times led to different labels for the two of them.

Laing's cases, as well as the Fitzgeralds, raises one question on the whole ignored by social reaction theory. Why do some people accept the labels? Why do the young women described by Laing not tell their parents that they, the parents, are crazy and leave home? Why did not

Zelda divorce Scott? There is clearly something special about the minds of those who get labeled crazy, but it is not psychiatric illness. Rather, it is perhaps a lack of self-confidence, maturity and independence that leads them to accept the label rather than rejecting it along with the labelers.

A Social Reaction Theory of Suicide

It is interesting that no social reaction theory of suicide has yet appeared. Despite the prominence of the perspective in criminology and its application to psychiatric disturbance over twenty-five years ago, it has had no impact on suicidology. This suggests that it might be provocative, and perhaps fruitful, to try to formulate a social reaction theory of suicide.

The first question to consider is whether people do indeed become labeled as "suicidal" and by whom. Some situations may be infrequent but likely situations for labeling. In those cases where a parent has committed suicide, people may worry that the spouse or the children of the suicide will likewise commit suicide. Today, there are many survivor groups specifically to help survivors work through their feelings about the suicide and to prevent them turning to suicide (Lukas and Seiden, 1987).

Let us imagine that the friends and relatives of these survivors, especially if they are children, are anxious about them becoming suicidal and are constantly on the lookout for suicidal cues. The children are very likely to pick up this anxiety and constant observation and to draw the obvious inference—they are worried that I will kill myself like Daddy did.

Relatives, parents and friends may even put this concern in words and, indeed, even label the child as a potential suicide. "If you don't watch it, you'll kill yourself just like your father." Peers at school can be particularly cruel. In a school in which three students committed suicide, many students in the school became suicidal in the following weeks. One student who attempted suicide found a bottle of Tylenol in her locker with a note saying, "Do it right next time" (Lester, 1987).

Thus, it is possible that informal labeling of individuals occurs in these situations.

Formal Labeling

Formal labeling can also occur. I remember working as a crisis counselor at a suicide prevention center and receiving a call from an individual who asked me, "Do I have to be suicidal to talk to you?" I was reminded of the situation in the USA before abortion was, to some extent, legalized. In some states, in order to have a legal abortion, a psychiatrist had to certify that the women would be seriously disturbed if an abortion was not permitted. In those states, informed women knew to threaten suicide if they had to have the child, whereupon the cooperating psychiatrist would have the required conditions to sign the appropriate forms.

Perhaps one has to appear and be labeled as suicidal in order to obtain certain things in a society and, after so appearing, perhaps the role becomes appealing?

The existence of suicide prevention centers, suicide prevention programs and suicide awareness programs all raise the possibility that you may be suicidal. An advertisement for a suicide prevention center informs people that suicide is an option. If you call or visit a suicide prevention center, are you now a "suicidal person?" When you watch a suicide prevention or awareness program in the media or at school, you learn the cues for recognizing suicidal preoccupation in others. These programs provide the direct learning of how to play the role that Scheff claims is necessary but is hard pressed to document for his theory of the development of psychiatric illness.

If you are in a psychiatric hospital or a jail or prison, the staff may become concerned about whether you might kill yourself and put you on "suicide alert." This means that potential methods for committing suicide will be taken from you and you will be monitored continuously. Might not being put on suicide alert actually increase the risk of your subsequent death by suicide at some point in your life? Labeling theory would argue so.

The effect of labeling may also account for the high rate of suicide among those who have attempted suicide (Lester, 1983). Perhaps attempting suicide and being admitted to the medical and psychiatric wards of a hospital, thereby earning the formal label of being "suicidal," is the critical factor resulting in a higher suicide rate rather than some characterological trait. It would be interesting to compare mortality in suicide attempters of equivalent lethality who are processed through institutions and so labeled and those who recover without institutional involvement.

Thus, it would appear that there are opportunities for learning the suicidal role in life and for being labeled, both informally and formally, as a potential suicide. Since there are such opportunities, it would seem important in future research to explore whether there is any evidence that such labeling occurs and leads to changes in the suicidal potential of the individuals so labeled.

The question of who accepts the label of being suicidal and who rejects it is important, too. What is the impact of being put on suicide alert in an institution of the individual's conception of himself or herself? Which kinds of people accept that they may be suicidal and who rejects the label? (Note that people who are truly suicidal may deny it to staff, and so simply asking a patient whether they are "suicidal" or not may not answer the question of whether they have or have not accepted the label.)

The Rewards From Being Labeled

Just as Braginsky et al. (1969) argued that psychiatric patients get rewards from accepting the label of being psychiatrically disturbed, in Chapter 5 we discussed how suicidal behavior may be shaped in individuals by the rewards that they get from being suicidal — attention, concern, perhaps even affection. The patient status has its rewards.

Research needs to be conducted on the ways in which being suicidal affects how others react toward you. What happens to a suicidal high school student? Who is made anxious by the student's suicidal status, who becomes hostile, but more importantly who becomes solicitous? Is there any status to being suicidal? Butscher (1976) in his biography of Sylvia Plath says that Sylvia had created a romantic aura for herself during her senior year at college as a result of her suicide attempt.

Stigma

An important area of research opened up by the labeling perspective concerned the stigma of being labeled. As Braginsky et al. (1969) pointed out, there is little stigma as long as you are with people like yourself. Psychiatric patients may feel stigma only when they are around ordinary people. Thus, the existence of stigma may increase the chances that suicidal and depressed individuals will form a separate peer group or n the larger society.

re is stigma to suicide has been documented. Kalish (1966)

gave a standard social distance scale to college students (would you da
this person, become close friends with him, let live on your street, and s
on). He found that much more social distance was placed between the
respondent and the hypothetical person if the hypothetical person was
an attempted suicide or an ex-psychiatric patient than if the hypothetical
person was black, Jewish, or Hispanic.

Discussion

Although little or no research has been conducted that is relevant to
this perspective, it is clear that this perspective raises several questions
that merit research, the results of which may surprise us.

Implications for Preventing Suicide

One of the standard ways of treating someone who has suffered a
trauma is to provide support and empathic listening and to reassure
them that everyone who experiences such a trauma feels the way they do
and that they are not going crazy. It also helps to get them back into the
situation from which the trauma removed them as quickly as possible.

For example, say a child almost drowns. If the child is not re-introduced
(in a safe way, of course) to water quite quickly, that child may develop a
fear of and perhaps a phobia of water.

In cases of soldiers who break down in combat, it was found that
removing them from the front, sedating them for a few days, followed by
a few days of rest and relaxation, after which they are returned to the
front, helped them overcome the trauma quickly and complete their
tour of duty satisfactorily (Kisker, 1984). Treating them as in need of
counseling and therapy, on the other hand, tended to turn them into
chronic psychiatric patients who received psychiatric discharges from
the service and who remained in psychiatric treatment for many years
afterwards.

The labeling perspective for delinquency led to recommendations for
diversion in order to reduce the risk of labeling and the consequence
that the individual will accept the label. If the same perspective is
applied to suicide, then we would want to minimize the labeling of
individuals as suicidal. Thus, suicide prevention centers might better be
labeled as crisis services, which has indeed happened to a large extent
in recent years, though not because of consideration of the labeling
perspective.

The labeling perspective suggests that putting inpatients or prisoners on "suicide alert" is not a good idea from the labeling perspective, though it may save the institution from liability should an inmate commit suicide.

The labeling perspective suggests that more general programs for improving psychological health in schools would be preferable to having programs which sensitize students specifically to suicide.

Thus, a social reaction theory of suicide would urge diversion of patients from suicide prevention programs and avoidance of labeling people as suicidal, a radically different approach from those traditionally taken with suicidal patients.

REFERENCES

Becker, H. *Outsiders.* New York: Macmillan, 1963.

Braginsky, B. M., Braginsky, D. D., & Ring, K. *Methods of madness.* New York: Holt, Rinehart & Winston, 1969.

Butscher, E. *Sylvia Plath.* New York: Seabury Press, 1976.

Critchlow, B. The powers of John Barleycorn. *American Psychologist,* 1986, 41, 751–764.

Kalish, R. A. Social distance and the dying. *Community Mental Health Journal,* 1966, 2, 152–155.

Kisker, G. W. *The disorganized personality.* New York: McGraw-Hill, 1984.

Laing, R. D., & Esterson, A. *Sanity, madness and the family.* New York: Basic Books, 1964.

Lemert, E. *Human deviance, social problems, and social control.* Englewood Cliffs, NJ: Prentice-Hall, 1967.

Lester, D. *Why people kill themselves.* Springfield, IL: Charles C Thomas, 1983.

Lester, D. *Suicide as a learned behavior.* Springfield, IL: Charles C Thomas, 1987.

Lukas, C., & Seiden, H. M. *Silent grief.* New York: Scribners, 1987.

MacAndrew, C., & Edgerton, R. B. *Drunken comportment.* Chicago: Aldine, 1969.

Marlatt, A., Demming, B., & Reid, J. Loss of control drinking in alcoholics. *Journal of Abnormal Psychology,* 1973, 81, 233–241.

Milford, N. *Zelda.* New York: Harper & Row, 1970.

Scheff, T. *Being mentally ill.* Chicago: Aldine, 1966.

Schur, E. *Radical nonintervention.* Englewood Cliffs, NJ: Prentice-Hall, 1973.

Sobell, L., Sobell, M., & Christelman, W. The myth of "one drink." *Behavior Therapy & Research,* 1972, 10, 119–123.

Chapter 8

A SOCIAL CONFLICT THEORY OF SUICIDE

Social conflict theories of crime focus on the ways that governments make and enforce laws both informally and formally. Might these laws simply be a way in which those in power maintain their power and control the oppressed in a society?

To illustrate the ways in which the elite in a society maintain their power, consider the educational system. If we were to take a group of four- or five-year-olds and let them be together unsupervised, we would witness a lot of spontaneous, often unruly, behavior. As soon as they enter the school system, their behavior becomes subject to control. They must learn to sit quietly, raise their hand if they want to talk, have a pass from the teacher to move about the building, and so on. When they enter high school, by which time a number of the children have dropped out, they are quite well behaved, but high school teachers still spend a considerable amount of time trying to maintain control. Sit down, stop talking, do this, don't do that.

The contrast between high school students and college students, by which time of course even more have dropped out, is dramatic. College teachers spend very little time maintaining order in the classroom. Those who will not conform have been dropped from the educational system by this time. Those who remain sit without fidgeting and without talking, dressed appropriately. They take notes, raise hands to ask questions, and soon learn never to disagree with what the professor believes. They graduate, perhaps with debts from the loans they took to pay for their undergraduate education, and, if they received high enough grades and expressed the appropriate sentiments on their graduate or professional school applications, were admitted for further education.

Here the costs increase and so do the size of the loans that have to be taken to pay for the education. The work increases in difficulty and the professors become harsher. Some professors grade the students on how well they critique the presentations made by their peers in the seminars. This strategy sets the students against one another and weakens any potential collaboration by the oppressed. Students are forced to work on research projects that are of interest to their professors, and any publications that result will have their professor's name on it—even the doctoral dissertation which is supposed to be an original, creative and independent work. Those in professional schools are expected to put in long hours at minimum pay to serve out their apprenticeships. It is difficult to rebel against this, since by now you have invested many years of your life and a great deal of money getting the degree you are seeking. Furthermore, to get a good first job, you need a recommendation from one of the professors/oppressors.

Is it any wonder that people graduate with a Ph.D. or an M.D. in their mid-twenties or later as clones of the educational elite, the academic professors who are in control of the educational system? The educational system is a wonderfully efficient agent of social control. It is very hard to come through it with creativity, spontaneity and any rebelliousness intact.

In the same way, laws and the criminal justice system serve the interests of those in power. The criminal justice system oppresses those without power and status in society and serves the interests only of those in power. The powerful seek to impose their conceptions of morality and their standards of behavior on society and to protect their property and power. To do this, they are usually able to draw the middle classes into this pattern of control, since maintenance of the control seems to serve middle-class interests as well.

According to this perspective, the poor, the lower classes and the oppressed do not commit more crimes than the oppressors. They are simply caught more often and punished more severely. Let us take a simple example which illustrates this.

Let us consider a poor lower-class citizen who takes a gun and robs a store owner of one thousand dollars. If caught, he will be convicted of a felony and serve a long term in prison. Let us consider one of the firms that provides armaments for the Pentagon. We have read in recent years of the government being charged thousands of dollars for parts which can be bought in stores for a few dollars. We have read of companies found guilty of defrauding the government on contracts for millions of dollars. What happens to the owners of these companies? Nothing. The company may be fined, but that simply comes out of profits. The dividend to shareholders might be reduced by a few pence. Has the chief executive officer of any of those companies paid a fine out of his own pocket, let alone gone to prison? Of course not.

In the recent oil spill in Alaska in 1989, the highest-ranking person in Exxon sentenced so far in court has been the captain of the ship. Or to take a very different example, as a result of all of the atrocities committed by Americans during their intervention in the civil war in Vietnam, the highest person charged and convicted was a lieutenant.

In 1990, Michael Milken pleaded guilty to just six counts of the 98 against him, including conspiracy and mail fraud. His fine was $600 million, though his personal fortune was estimated to be over $1 billion. Speculation was that $400 million of the fine may be tax deductible (Greenwald, 1990). Milken might be sentenced to five years in prison, but federal prisons are often called "Club Feds" to indicate that they are more like holidays than comparable time spent at a state prison. If I were poor and unemployed and serving ten years in state prison for a robbery netting a few thousand dollars, I would be angry.

Most social conflict theorists of crime are Westerners, so they often attack the capitalist system in their theories. A social conflict theory of crime could be applied just as easily to communist dictatorships. Stalin and Brezhnev in the Soviet Union or Mao Tse Tung and, now, Li Peng in the People's Republic of China have been exceedingly skilled in using the criminal justice system to maintain the status of the elite in power, despite supposedly having a Marxist ideology at the basis of their system of government which is opposed to oppression.

Sykes (1974) has argued that the rules imposed by the ruling classes have little relationship to the cultural norms of the poor. In a society where affluence is well-publicized and becomes a major goal for people, frustration is bound to be generated in those who cannot attain and share in this affluence. The have-nots, therefore, develop a deep-rooted hostility toward the social order.

Schwendinger and Schwendinger (1979) argued that the legal system in the United States serves to secure an economic system that is centered around capitalism and guards the position of the owners at the expense of the workers. Many of the support systems, such as the education system, are designed to secure the labor force. (We might note that keeping people in school reduces the level of unemployment by removing students from the labor market. It also secures appropriate numbers of professionals trained to serve industry and sufficient numbers of civil servants.) Because of the antagonism built into the capitalist system, the legal system can never achieve its stated purpose of producing justice.

It is interesting to note that organizations set up to help the workers often become corrupted in their aims. The high levels of oppression in the so-called Marxist countries is good evidence of this. In our world, however, unions, which initially did much to liberate the worker from abuse at the hands of the owners, eventually became rigid organizations whose leaders were often corrupt and who abused the workers they represented. In a more subtle diversion, union-run pension plans now invest their enormous funds in shares of the major companies, so that the well-being of the capitalists is tied to the well-being of the union workers.

Quinney's (1970) conlict model is less tied to a critique of any particular governing system. Quinney suggested that crime is a definition of human conduct that is created by authorized agents in any politically organized society. These definitions describe behaviors that conflict with the interests of those segments of society which shape public policy. The definitions are applied by those segments of society which have the power to shape the criminal justice system. The less power your segment of society has, the greater the chance that your behavior patterns will be defined as criminal, and thus the greater the likelihood you will violate the criminal law.

Quinney suggested that conceptions of crime are diffused through society by the channels of communication. This means that, today, those seeking to change society often propose alternative definitions of crime and seek to diffuse these new definitions through the same communication channels. During America's intervention in the Vietnam civil war, anti-war groups defined those running the war as the real criminals. Ecology groups define industry as the real criminal. However, these redefinitions have to compete against those held by the majority and so are often disregarded, though in both examples given above the redefinitions eventually had a significant impact on the ruling segments of society.

There is an important distinction between Marxist conflict theories and other conflict theories (Vold, 1979). In the Marxist perspective, criminal behavior may be still be seen as pathological, but it is attributed to the pathological nature of capitalist society. Since the workers are denied a productive role in society, they become demoralized and act in criminal ways. If society was more socialist, the workers would be less oppressed and criminal behavior would become less frequent. Other conflict criminologists, however, consider criminal behavior to be the normal actions of normal people who have insufficient power to control the criminalization process.

In the social conflict view, therefore, criminals are really "political criminals," and the solution to the crime problem is to reform society. The oppression of one segment by another segment must be stopped and, unlike what has happened in previous attempts to do this, not simply replaced by alternative types of oppression. Social conflict theorists, therefore, would urge the elimination of racism, sexism, and other forms of oppression through a social revolution.

A Social Conflict Theory of Suicide: Suicide as a Political Act

Suicide can, of course, be a political act. People have killed themselves in order to publicize some cause and to attempt to bring about some change. For example, the Buddhist monk Thich Quang Duc immolated himself in Saigon on June 11, 1963, as a protest against the regime of Ngo Dinh Diem in South Vietnam, following which other people immolated themselves in Vietnam, the USA and elsewhere to protest the political situation in Vietnam (Coleman, 1987).

However, suicide can be conceptualized more broadly as a political act, using the word "politics" in the sense that Laing (1967) uses the word to describe any behavior in which one or more people exert power over others. Writers such as Haley (1969) and Laborit (1970) have argued forcefully that the desire for power and for dominating others may be one of the more powerful desires motivating human behavior, and its effects can be documented quite clearly in suicidal behavior where the suicidal act can easily change the power balance in relationships.

Attempted suicide has long been seen as a manipulative act (Sifneos, 1966; Lester, 1968). The attempted suicide is often trying to force certain responses from significant others. Perhaps the lover about to leave you will stay? Perhaps he or she will pay attention to your distress? A threat of suicide can have equally powerful effects on significant others in changing their immediate response to the threatener.

Menninger (1938) described three motives in the suicidal act: to die, anger directed toward oneself, and anger directed toward others. This latter motive often manifests itself in obvious efforts to exert power over others. The person who shoots himself, for example, in front of significant others, or in such a way that they discover him, clearly wants to traumatize them and shape the memory they have of him. The person may be trying to leave the survivors with guilt, and the stigma that attaches to the survivors of suicides adds to their trauma (Rudestam, 1977).

The efforts of the suicide may not always be directed to causing others pain. Antigone, in Sophocles's play of the same name, is trying to restore honor to the name of her family and glory to herself by her suicidal actions (Faber, 1970), and Japanese officials who commit suicide often do so for similar reasons of honor. By trying to shape how others will experience them, they are behaving politically in Laing's sense of the word.

Counts (1988) too has documented how suicide may be used to change one's image in the social group. In Papua, New Guinea, suicide often acts as a form of social sanction. It has political consequences for the surviving kin and for those who are held responsible for the events precipitating the suicide. Counts relates a case of Agnes, a woman who tried to seduce Victor into marriage and against whom the whole village turned. Victor's family rejected her as a bride and she killed herself. Her suicide changed the feeling in the village, and now Victor and his family were seen to be at fault. Whereas Victor's family had refused to pay Agnes a bridal fee, they were now willing to pay her kin compensation. Victor's kin now faced both the disgrace of having caused Agnes's death and the financial loss. Agnes also removed her shame by killing herself. This case shows nicely the dual aspects in the suicidal act of freeing oneself while oppressing others. (Such freeing of oneself may be the underlying motive in cases of *fatalistic* suicide [Durkheim, 1897].)

In another vein, Meerloo (1962) has described *psychic homicide* in which a person commits murder by getting someone else to commit suicide. More recent cases have been described by Richman (1986) in his cases of suicide taking place in the context of a family, in which members covertly, and sometimes overtly, communicate and "force" one family member to kill himself.

Thus, in the many ways described here, suicide may be conceptualized as a political act in which the suicidal person seeks to change the balance of power in his social group or more broadly in society.

Suicide and Sexist Views

For many years now, suicidologists have classified suicidal acts in which the person dies as *completed suicide* and those in which the person survives as *attempted suicide*. Since it was realized that many of those attempting suicide do not intend to die (they often make gestures such as delicate wrist cuts or knowingly take non-lethal amounts of medications), European suicidologists have switched to calling attempted suicides *parasuicides* and more recently as *self-injurers* and *self-poisoners*.

The basic sex difference in suicide is that more men complete suicide than women while more women attempt suicide than men (Lester, 1984). For example, in one of the most comprehensive community surveys conducted in this country, Farberow and Shneidman (1961) located 540 men and 228 women in Los Angeles County in 1957 who had completed suicide and 828 men and 1824 women who had attempted suicide. It is clear that women engaged in more suicidal actions than men, and this difference is probably much greater since the community survey failed to count those making suicide attempts that did not come to the attention of the caretakers in the community.

The extent to which this information has permeated society and has led to gender-based expectations was demonstrated by Linehan (1973). She presented students with case vignettes and asked them to predict the likelihood of completed suicide. Completed suicide was predicted more often as the outcome for male patients than for female patients, and also as more likely for masculine patients than for feminine patients.

Indeed, Douglas (1967), in a critique of the use of official statistics on completed suicide, argued that female completed suicides may be concealed more than male completed suicides by those involved in the certification of the death, partially in order to free the male survivors from responsibility of having driven their wife (or mother) to suicide.

But let us look at this phenomenon from the female point of view. The statistically normal result is to live after the suicidal action. But by naming the acts in which people die as *completed* implies that dying constitutes a successful act while attempting constitutes a failure of some kind. If we let numbers guide us, then surviving is the norm and dying is deviant.

We could introduce a reverse bias by calling attempted suicides *successful suicides* and completed suicides *failed suicides*. Those who are dead failed because they died. But perhaps we could eliminate bias by calling all

suicides and merely appending dead (or deceased) and living as
al modifiers?

this transformation, some old research findings make more sense.
For example, Shneidman and Farberow (1957) described what they felt
was the faulty logic of the dead suicide. They felt that he or she confused
the self as experienced by the self with the self as experienced by others.
The dead suicide often acted as if he or she would be around after the act
to witness (and enjoy) the reactions of others to the suicide. Shneidman
and Farberow called this faulty logic *catalogic.*

With our reverse bias, in which attempted suicide is the norm and less
deviant act, it is clear that living suicides are present to enjoy the
reactions of others to their suicidal act, and thus they are not guilty of
faulty logic. Catalogic is characteristic only of failed (dead) suicidal
people.

Theories of Suicide

The sociological study of suicide appears to have been stimulated,
legitimized and subsequently beholden to Durkheim's (1897) seminal
work. Very few studies of suicide today are published without mention of
Durkheim's ideas, and the studies typically use Durkheim's ideas as the
theoretical basis for the study.

Durkheim studied only completed suicide with the result that later
sociologists have rarely studied attempted suicide, an omission that has
been criticized by Wilkins (1967) and more recently by Taylor (1982).

There is no such bias in psychology/psychiatry, probably for two
reasons. First, whereas sociological research employs official statistics of
completed suicide, psychologists prefer to have "subjects" to whom psychological tests are administered. Thus, psychologists have turned to the
study of attempted suicides because they are available for interview.

Second, attempted suicide is a common and life-threatening psychiatric symptom. As such, it merits and receives a great deal of attention
from psychiatrists. Third, psychologists see suicide as primarily a symptom of depressed patients, and depression too is considered a serious
syndrome worthy of study. The sociological study of attempted suicide
and depression has been hindered by the difficulty of calculating rates of
these behaviors in different societies. However, Lester (1989a) located
some epidemiological studies of attempted suicide which provided the
basic information required by sociologists. He also presented some tenta-

tive sociological theories of attempted suicide in order to stimulate other sociologists to focus upon this behavior.

Reactions to Suicide

It has been well documented that emergency-room personnel are quite hostile toward attempted suicides (who are, remember, mainly women). These personnel resent the time "wasted" on the care of these patients while medically sick people also await attention (Dressler et al., 1975).

Our reactions to completed suicides are different. For those of us who have contemplated suicide, the suicide's death arouses our anxiety and sympathy. Our prejudice is more likely to be directed toward the *survivors* of the completed suicide as we wonder what these survivors did to drive the person to take his or her own life (Rudestam, 1989).

This hostility toward the suicide attempter is perhaps reflective of our bias that completed suicide is the appropriate behavior and that attempting suicide is merely a nuisance. Suicide attempters are not *serious* in their intent. Supervisory staff of hospitals and clinics must deal with these inappropriate hostile attitudes toward attempted suicides. It is no less a problem when scholars seem to share such attitudes but harder to devise solutions.

Discussion

This section has suggested how an initial effort might be made to transform the study of suicide by eliminating the sexist bias present in the existing terminology and the typical focus of interest. The historic focus on completed suicide as a topic worthy of study, and the comparative neglect of attempted suicide except as a step on the way to an eventual suicidal death, has been discussed and an alternative focus suggested. Not only is attempted suicide a more common behavior, it may be more rational and more adaptive. Rather than death *completing* the suicidal act, it may signal *failure* of the act. Further thought along the lines may help to truly transform the study of suicide and our understanding of the behavior.

Modernization and Suicide Rates

A social conflict theory of suicide would predict that suicide should be more common in modern (capitalist) societies. Morselli (1882) made such a suggestion, as did DeCatanzaro (1981). DeCatanzaro felt that this might be due to the fact that primitive societies are less technologically advanced and so lack easy ways for committing suicide. However, hanging and drowning are relatively simple and easily available ways for committing suicide and available to those in primitive societies.

It appears that there is a large variation in the suicide rates of primitive societies, ranging from a rate of 23 per 100,000 per year in Kandrian (New Guinea) (Hoskin et al., 1969) to zero among the Zuni in America (Lester, 1987). However, anthropologists studying primitive societies are studying them in the twentieth century, long after the colonial powers had influenced these societies. Thus, primitive societies may have had low suicide rates before the colonial powers arrived and interfered.

Stack and Danigelis (1985) examined the effect of modernization on suicide rates in seventeen nations of the world (all of which were capitalist) from 1919 to 1974. They found that modernization led on the whole to relatively greater female suicide rates while not affecting male suicide rates much at all. The net result was a decrease in the male/female suicide rate ratio.

Racism and Suicide

In nations with white oppressors and black oppressed, it has been documented that suicide rates are higher for the whites while homicide rates are higher for the blacks (Lester, 1989b). However, Hendin (1982) documented high rates of suicide among urban young black males in the USA. Hendin found that they had been exposed to family and peer violence, but that they also lived in disastrous social conditions, experiencing the bitterness and disappointments of ghetto life. Hendin felt that the culture's overt rejection of black people in the ghetto reinforced their feelings of anger and worthlessness already present as a result of their upbringing. Hendin suggested, in addition, that the cultural rejection of blacks is one of the reasons why black adults are such poor parents to their children, for their own rage and feelings of worthlessness prevent them from being effective parents.

Hendin noted that the young blacks he studied felt trapped in an unalterable life situation by their lack of education and lack of job opportunities and by the destructive effect of the ghetto on their own personalities.

Culture influences character by a complex psychodynamic process in which culturally induced family patterns play a key role in perpetuating problems. The rage and self-hatred that are integral parts of the black family situation in the ghetto are inseparable from the rage and self-hatred that are the outgrowths of racial discrimination in a society that stimulates the desires of blacks but blocks their fulfillment. (P. 93.)

Job Loss and Suicide

A standard component of the economic situation of capitalist nations is that there is unemployment. Reasonable rates of unemployment keep wages down and so reduce the costs of manufacturing goods, and there are economic dangers to having too low rates of unemployment.

The evidence is overwheleming that unemployment is associated with high rates of suicide. Platt (1984) in a review of the research literature found that suicides more often had a history of job loss and job instability than non-suicides and, in addition, the unemployed have a higher risk of subsequent suicide.

The methodology of the research does not permit us to draw cause-and-effect conclusions. It may be that unemployment itself increases the risk of suicide, but it may be also that some other factor (such as psychiatric disturbance) increases the chances of both unemployment and suicide, thereby leading to the association between unemployment and suicide. Nonetheless, the association between unemployment and suicide is consistent with an indictment of the capitalist system.

Does Your Life Belong To You?

Interestingly, many types of governments have maintained that we do not have the right to commit suicide since our life does not belong to us. In the Christian view, God gives us life and so only God can take it away. In totalitarian societies, your life belonged to the King, to the owner of the serfs, and, in communist nations, to the state.

Only in recent times has consideration been given to the possibility that we may have a right to die, and perhaps to kill ourselves since our lives belong to us (Beloff, 1989). As this view becomes more entrenched in law, it would appear that we may have finally become free from this particular form of oppression.

Implications for Suicide Prevention

The implications of the social conflict theory of suicide for prevention are simple to state but difficult to implement. Oppression in all its forms must be eliminated. People must not be oppressed because of religious, ethnic, gender, class or age characteristics. Governments should take as their major goal the facilitation of the self-actualization of every one of the members of society.

The problem, of course, is that modern societies are so complex that changes in one area have impacts in others. We have witnessed in recent months that liberation from communist dictatorships in Eastern European nations has led to increases in nationalism, ethnic conflicts, antisemitism, higher prices (which leads to an increase in poverty), and higher rates of unemployment. Increasing the opportunities for one group of society often is associated with reducing the opportunities for other groups.

Sometimes, supporting a group endeavoring to escape from tyranny is not simple. Some Marxists support the struggles of the Palestinians in their fight for autonomy, while recognizing that women's rights will suffer greatly under traditional male Arabic rule.

Are suicide rates lower in Marxist governments? In my opinion there are no modern Marxist governments, though there are communist dictatorships. So we do not know what the patterns of suicidal behavior would be under a Marxist government. However, there is certainly no evidence that the patterns of suicidal behavior are different under communist dictatorships. East Germany, when it published its suicide rate, reported a suicide rate higher than that of West Germany. (In 1970 East Germany reported a rate of 30.5 per 100,000 per year versus 21.3 in West Germany. East Germany stopped reporting suicide rates after 1974.) Hungary has had the highest suicide rate in the world of any modern nation for several decades (34.8 in 1970). So our answer must be in the negative. Communist governments have not witnessed low suicide rates.

REFERENCES

Beloff, J. Do we have a right to die? In A. Berger, P. Badham, A. H. Kutscher, J. Berger, M. Perry, & J. Beloff (Eds.), *Perspectives on death and dying.* Philadelphia: Charles Press, 1989, pp. 163–172.

Coleman, L. *Suicide clusters.* Boston: Faber & Faber, 1987.

Counts. D. A. Ambiguity in the interpretation of suicide. In D. Lester (Ed.), *Why women kill themselves.* Springfield: Charles C Thomas, 1988, pp. 87–109.

DeCatanzaro, D. *Suicide and self-damaging behavior.* New York: Academic Press, 1981.

Douglas. J. D. *The social meanings of suicide.* Princeton: Princeton University Press, 1967.

Dressler, D. M., Prussof, B., Hark, H., & Shapiro, D. Clinician attitudes toward the suicide attempter. *Journal of Nervous & Mental Disease,* 1975, 160, 146–155.

Durkheim, E. *Le Suicide.* Paris: Felix Alcan, 1897.

Faber, M. D. *Suicide and Greek tragedy.* New York: Sphinx, 1970.

Farberow, N. L., & Shneidman, E. S. *The cry for help.* New York: McGraw-Hill, 1961.

Greenwald, J. Baby, you're a rich man still. *Time,* 1990, 135(20), 72.

Haley, J. *The power tactics of Jesus Christ and other essays.* New York: Grossman, 1969.

Hendin, H. *Suicide in America.* New York: Norton, 1982.

Hoskin, J., Friedman, M., & Cawte, J. A high incidence of suicide in a pre-literate primitive society. *Psychiatry,* 1969, 32, 200–210.

Laborit. H. *L'homme imaginant.* Paris: Union General d'Editions, 1970.

Laing, R. D. *The politics of experience.* New York: Pantheon, 1967.

Lester, D. Attempted suicide as a hostile act. *Journal of Psychology,* 1968, 68, 243–248.

Lester, D. Suicide. In C. S. Widom (Ed.), *Sex roles and psychopathology.* New York: Plenum, 1984, pp. 145–156.

Lester, D. *Suicide as a learned behavior.* Springfield, IL: Charles C Thomas, 1987.

Lester, D. *Sociological perspectives on suicide.* Springfield: Charles C Thomas, 1989a.

Lester, D. Personal violence (suicide and homicide) in South Africa. *Acta Psychiatrica Scandinavia,* 1989b, 79, 235–237.

Linehan, M. Suicide and attempted suicide. *Perceptual & Motor Skills,* 1973, 37, 31–34.

Meerloo, J. A. M. *Suicide and mass suicide.* New York: Grune & Stratton, 1962.

Menninger, K. *Man against himself.* New York: Harcourt Brace & World, 1938.

Morselli, H. *Suicide.* New York: Appleton, 1882.

Platt, S. Unemployment and suicidal behavior. *Social Science & Medicine,* 1984, 19, 93–115.

Quinney, R. *The social reality of crime.* Boston: Little Brown, 1970.

Richman, J. *Family therapy for suicidal people.* New York: Springer, 1986.

Rudestam, K. E. Physical and psychological responses to suicide in the family. *Journal of Consulting & Clinical Psychology,* 1977, 45, 162–170.

Rudestam, K. E. Survivors of suicide. In D. Lester (Ed.), *Understanding suicide: the state of the art.* Philadelphia: Charles Press, 1989.

Schwendinger, H., & Schwendinger, J. Delinquency and social reform. In L. Empey (Ed.), *Juvenile justice.* Charlottesville, VA: University of Virginia Press, 1979, pp. 246–290.

Shneidman, E. S., & Farberow, N. L. The logic of suicide. In E. S. Shneidman & N. L. Farberow (Eds.), *Clues to suicide.* New York: McGraw-Hill, 1957, pp. 31–40.

Sifneos, P. Manipulative suicide. *Psychiatric Quarterly,* 1966, 40, 525–537.

Stack, S., & Danigelis, N. Modernization and the sex differential in suicide, 1919–1972. *Comparative Social Research,* 1985, 8, 203–216.

Sykes, G. The rise of critical criminology. *Journal of Criminal Law & Criminology,* 1974, 22, 335–347.

Taylor, S. *Durkheim and the study of suicide.* London: Macmillan, 1982.

Vold, G. B. *Theoretical criminology.* New York: Oxford University Press, 1979.

Wilkins, J. Suicidal behavior. *American Sociological Review,* 1967, 32, 286–298.

Chapter 9

CONCLUSIONS

The goal of this book has been to suggest new theories of suicide and to explore their implications for preventing suicide. The source of these new theories was the research and theory-building of those who have studied deviance and crime, for it appeared that those interested in suicide have neglected the strategies of those concerned with other personal and social problems. Let us first present a brief summary of what was accomplished here.

The New Theories

A Classicial Theory of Suicide

A classical theory of suicide viewed suicide as a rational decision made by an individual who weighs the costs and benefits of suicide versus other alternative actions. This viewpoint in suicide has rarely been proposed. However, Yang, an economist, has proposed a cost-benefit and a demand-supply analysis of suicide which is based upon such a viewpoint. In addition, Clarke and Lester have argued that the choice of a method for suicide is a rational choice based upon the effects of different methods on the body and on the mind.

Prevention techniques based on this viewpoint involve increasing the costs of suicide and decreasing the benefits. I have suggested that public education programs should emphasize the possibilities of disfigurement and long-term physical disability after an unsuccessful suicide attempt as well as the pain experienced by survivors of a suicide. Although, of course, it would be pointless to make suicide illegal, I have suggested that the various religious and moral authorities, many of whom hold suicide to be a sin, should come out as strongly opposed to suicide as they do for other life-and-death issues such as abortion.

Related to this, Clarke and Lester (1989) found in their research that making a lethal method for suicide less readily available, not only decreased its use for suicide, but sometimes decreased the overall suicide rate as well. As a result of their research, they advocated making lethal methods for suicide less available.

Tactics based upon their suggestion would include fencing-in bridges from which people jump, stricter gun control laws, restricting the size of prescriptions and putting lethal medications in plastic blisters. These measures would increase the difficulty of committing suicide, that is, increase the cost. Critics of this position argue that people would simply switch methods for suicide. Clarke and Lester have responded by noting that there is no good evidence that they will, that even if they do they may switch to less lethal methods (pills are less lethal than guns), and that even if they do switch methods we still have a responsibility to prevent death from easily available implements. After all, we are required to fence-in swimming pools in our backyards to prevent neighborhood children from accidentally drowning even though those children may die accidentally in other locales.

A Positivist Individualistic Theory of Suicide

Positivist individualistic theories of suicide include the majority of psychological and psychiatric theories proposed so far to account for suicide. Such theories look for the causes of suicide in the individual's physiological constitution, psychological characteristics and psychiatric state.

Most of the already-existing suicide prevention strategies stem from this perspective. Psychiatric treatment, primarily with antidepressant medication, and psychotherapy have been recommended for already-suicidal individuals. In the last few decades, many suicide prevention centers, based on a crisis model of intervention, have sprung up around the country, mainly relying on telephone contact between a distressed suicidal client and a paraprofessional counselor.

A Social Structure Theory of Suicide

Two variants of social structure theory were proposed. In a culture deviance theory, it was suggested that there exist suicidal subcultures, especially in small communities such as schools, psychiatric hospitals and prisons, or native American reservations. These subcultures have different values and attitudes from the mainstream culture.

In addition, more broad subcultural patterns were described, such as the use of guns to solve problems (in both murder and suicide), which characterize whole regions. For example, it has long been true that Hungary has the highest suicide rate of any nation in the world. In addition, Hungarian immigrants to other nations have the highest suicide rates of all immigrant groups. Perhaps Hungarians have a subculture which makes suicide more likely?

Strain theories focus on the emotional experiences of those who have difficulty working toward the culturally approved goals by socially acceptable means. Those who fail in this task will experience anger, frustration and despair. They become retreatists, to use Robert Merton's set of types, perhaps episodically.

Prevention techniques stemming from this perspective focus on primary prevention, an unusual approach for those in suicide prevention. Programs which draw the members of deviant subcultures and the episodic retreatists into the school and college programs and into community organizations would go far in preventing suicide as well as other deviant styles of adaptation (such as drug abuse and delinquency). Indeed, it was possible to identify some school suicide prevention programs which have realized that this approach might work, although it was not possible to find specific proposals as to how this might be accomplished.

If we model suicide prevention programs on the crime and delinquency prevention programs, we would simply try to improve the community and its component organizations in general, and the decrease in suicidal and depressed behavior would follow as one of the side effects.

A Learning Theory of Suicide

Learning theories of suicide have been proposed only quite recently. Lester (1987) presented a convincing case that learning factors may play a strong role in the appearance of suicide in distressed individuals. Related to learning theories, a neutralization theory of suicide focusses on the ways in which the potential suicide neutralizes the inhibitions against killing himself. Interestingly, very little research has been conducted on this latter issue, and it would appear to merit more intensive study in the future. If we could find how people decrease their inhibitions against committing suicide, we might obtain some ideas as to how these inhibitions might be increased.

The prevention strategies stemming from the learning perspective focussed on how to deal with situations in which suicide occurs and from which others might learn about the behavior. In the chapter on learning theories of suicide, the discussion focussed primarily on groups for the close friends and relatives of suicide (the so-called survivor groups) in which the survivors are helped to cope with their feelings.

However, other proposals may be made based upon this perspective. For example, since media publicity of suicide appears to lead to an increase in suicide in the following week, care should be taken by the media in how they present the news about suicides so that learning is minimized. For example, details of the method used and how it was obtained are perhaps dangerous. Glamorizing the suicide is likely to increase the suggestive impact of the suicide on others. Furthermore, researchers in the field have suggested that the media always accompany suicide stories with information about the suicide prevention resources in the community.

Epidemics of suicide in institutions are often contained by isolating the suicidal individuals from the main body of the institution, so that the contagion effect can be minimized.

Interestingly, Lester (1989) has suggested a theory of suicide that bodes ill for preventing suicide from a learning perspective. Lester proposed a critical-mass theory of suicide in which, once suicide becomes sufficiently common in a society, then members of the society are very likely to have contact with suicides and thereby learn about the behavior. On the basis of this theory, Lester predicted and found that, during the 1970s, countries with the highest suicide rates experienced the greatest increases in their suicide rate.

A Social Control Theory of Suicide

A social control theory of suicide focusses on the social bonds and internal controls which prevent people from committing suicide. The major sociological theory of suicide, that proposed by Durkheim, fits here. Durkheim proposed that social integration and social regulation, in moderation, both served to make suicide less likely. Thus, increased social bonding should make suicide less likely. Psychological theories of suicide too have recognized the importance of social bonds—good relationships with parents, spouse and lovers, children and friends.

One variant of the social control theories, containment theory, focusses in addition on the internal forces that inhibit the appearance of suicidal behavior, such as strong ego strength and a positive self-image, belief in an internal locus of control, and good frustration tolerance and low impulsivity.

The prevention techniques that arise from this perspective are many. First, primary prevention could be advanced by promoting social bonding in the community and in institutions such as schools. Although such programs will never be initiated simply to prevent suicide, the effects of such programs are widespread, decreasing involvement in all types of deviant behavior, including drug abuse and delinquency. School programs are especially important, and the importance of school programs for primary prevention of deviance was also emphasized under the social structure perspective for suicide discussed above.

From an individual point of view, family therapy would appear to be the sine qua non for helping the suicidal individual, but it is often difficult to motivate the whole family to seek therapy. Group therapy may also be useful, but the social control perspective for suicide suggests the usefulness of social networking groups for suicidal individuals, that is, groups whose function would be to provide social experiences for the members, thereby building up their social ties.

A Social Reaction Theory of Suicide

A social reaction theory of suicide focusses on the ways in which people might be labeled as "suicidal" in the society and how they react to this labeling. Do they reject it or do they accept it and enter the career of being suicidal?

It was noted that putting patients on suicide alert in institutions (in order to monitor them more closely so as to prevent suicide) may result in labeling, as might clients deciding to call a suicide prevention center. Suicide education programs may introduce people to the suicidal career and show them how to proceed in the career.

Prevention in this perspective would involve diversion, that is, treatment of the suicidal person without labeling them as suicidal. The naming of those clinics which are set up to help suicidal people may be critical, and it was suggested that "crisis service" is better than "suicide prevention center" as a name. General psychological health programs in school may be more appropriate than awareness programs that focus on suicide.

A Social Conflict Theory of Suicide

A social conflict theory of suicide views suicide as the result of oppression of one group in society by another group. Evidence was produced which suggested the role that suicide played in manipulating the power balance in their relationship by oppressed individuals. Possible sexist biases in suicidology were also discussed.

It was suggested that modernization along capitalist lines might increase the risk of suicide, but the evidence for this was not strong yet. However, Hendin has argued that the oppression resulting from racism and social class may play a role in the high rates of suicide in young urban black males.

Suicide prevention in this perspective would involve reducing the oppression in people's lives, both from the larger social forces and from individual interpersonal relationships.

Discussion

Seven perspectives were presented in this volume for viewing suicidal behavior. Although elements of some of these perspectives have appeared in recent years, only two of the perspectives (individualistic positivist and social control) have any substantial parallels in standard suicide theorizing.

Two of the perspectives were completely new. Virtually no consideration has been given by suicidologists to social reaction and social conflict perspectives. We are not arguing here that such perspectives will assume great importance in the future. Rather, we are suggesting that consideration of the perspectives presented here may stimulate new research into the etiology of suicidal behavior.

We have tried to illustrate the potential of these perspectives by illustrating their implications for prevention. It was readily apparent, first of all, that the perspectives do indeed suggest new strategies for preventing suicide, ranging from community action programs to setting up social networks for suicidal people.

Second, it was also apparent that these perspectives provide a rationale for primary prevention, preventing the appearance of suicidal behavior in people, rather than intervening once the people have become suicidal. Again, this led to the realization that suicidologists have neglected primary prevention.

Armed with the perspectives presented in this book, we may move far toward understanding and preventing suicide in the twenty-first century.

REFERENCES

Clarke, R. V., & Lester, D. *Suicide: closing the exits.* New York: Springer-Verlag, 1989.

Lester, D. *Suicide as a learned behavior.* Springfield, IL: Charles C Thomas, 1987.

Lester, D. *Suicide from a sociological perspective.* Springfield, IL: Charles C Thomas, 1989.

AUTHOR INDEX

SUBJECT INDEX